Ari

FRANK KUPPNER was born in G
ever since. He has published sev
Second Best Moments in Chinese History was awarded a Scottish Arts
Council Book award in 1997. A novelist as well as a poet, he
received the McVitie's Prize for his fiction in 1995.

FRANK KUPPNER

Arioflotga

Being a revised index of first lines of
The Great Anthology

CARCANET

First published in Great Britain in 2008 by
Carcanet Press Limited
Alliance House
Cross Street
Manchester M2 7AQ

A CIP catalogue record for this book is available from the British Library
ISBN 978 1 85754 933 1

The publisher acknowledges financial assistance from Arts Council England

Typeset by XL Publishing Services, Tiverton
Printed and bound in England by SRP Ltd, Exeter

I have only had glimpses of the life I would like to have had. But that, I dare say, IjklmnO, is all I would have anyway.

[Please note that this is the revised list. Most of the doubtful ones have now been safely removed. Some better translations have been added. Dig out the original page and volume numbers, will you, and have them re-ordered accordingly. That shouldn't be too difficult, even for you. Technology can do anything these days. I don't have them myself and I'm far too busy anyway. A life's work, for what it's worth. I should be off home soon. Many thanks. More later, if absolutely necessary. Very few remain to be added. Get rid of this. By the way, why do you never visit me these days? Not that it matters all that much.]

A,b,c,d and so on. Where's the problem?
A beautiful dead girl drew the blinds aside;
A beautiful garden, with someone to talk to attached to it,
A beloved land is that central land, Oblivia with its marvels;
Abortion among the star-studs! Rape too! Ah, how rapturously
About failure on such a scale there is almost something heroic.
Above all else, God likes us to lie about dozing in the morning;
Above all else, the desire to be Oblivian.
Abraham – a completely imaginary figure –
"A brave literary academic?" Are you serious?
"Absolute shit"? Whenever I hear the phrase,
Absorbed as I was by a volume of Heraclitus in Sanskrit,
According to Mark, one of the brothers of Jesus was called Judas;
A clerical assistant, who hailed from distant San Ignacio,
A contradiction in terms with delusions of grandeur
A cry of, "Deaf, inconsiderate oaf!" woke me up again.
Actually, I understand women perfectly.
Actually, it doesn't smell too bad now.
Actually, it's pomegranate juice. Quite nice, no?
Adamson! I had supposed you were my friend.
A devout Christian alcoholic? Is that even possible?
Adios! The Gods are simply too expensive.
A disembodied voice whispering "F——k off!"
A dog barked, and the whole thing completely fell to pieces.
A few thousand more corpses were washed ashore that evening;
A few years ago, I was half a potato – when, suddenly
A flair for falling asleep in all the great temple sites
A flock of vicuña leisurely passing by
A friend of yours once told me you worship my stupidity. (Do you?)
After a fall in his home at the age of ten months
After a few shrill screams, the Stepson of God
After a second fall in his home at the age of ninety-one,
After a while, one simply packs it in and dies.
After God made your mole, Madam, I suspect He, quite justifiably,
After having had seven, or maybe eight, children – or maybe nine –

After I have ceased to exist, I just *know* I will still exist.
After joking for several years about having a heart problem,
After my last bowel operation, I said to myself: Ithuriel,
After our disastrous first meeting,
After sitting with one of her feet in my lap for most of the morning,
After sitting with one of her hands on my head for most of the
    evening,
After the brightest point of the day, something even brighter
After the proud traditional cry of, "It lacketh testicles!"
After the sudden delightful shower on Busch Avenue
A gay shadow pissing through the doors at evening
A great religious leader will soon come out of Alexandria
A group of water-drinking North American homosexuals
A half-decent pair of headlights quietly at work in a kitchen
Ah! Here it is at last! You know, I was almost beginning
Ah, yes! The old dream of absolute non-contingency!
A hymn of joy is rising again from the clean bathroom;
A ladder taller than the tree it was leaning against
A lady journalist from Thailand with utterly charming toes
A large, weathered shape at the back, which may be Jesus Christ,
Alas! Considered as a possible haven,
Alas, I am far too intelligent for my own good.
Alas, I have been quite unable to achieve satisfaction
Alas, I must rise and go now, and try my nightly couch;
Alas, I overlooked the fact that I too would grow old.
Alas, it is already clear to me that my son is a venomous little turd.
Alas, it seems they are merely a religious phenomenon –
Alas, my dear mother seems to have gone somewhat insane again.
Alas, not a single word of all that utterly marvellous teaching
Alas, the angel next door no longer flashes her wings at me.
Alas, the arrival of a younger ponce in a bigger car
A law-abiding citizen once found a hand-grenade
Alcohol? Surely alcohol is for sexual failures?
Alexander von Humboldt! Huh. We all know why
A lift climbs slowly in the hollow of my eyes
A little less melodrama, if you please, Penelope.
Allah does not like hearing the word 'Allah'.
Allah leads into error whomsoever he pleases
All art is a dulled nostalgia for our childhood toys;
All a writer can do today is fart uncontrollably.

All day in this retreat I hear the sound of bad men laughing;
All jewellery is a homage to the privatest of parts
All joys, all passions, all finer thoughts of Oblivia,
All languages compare badly even with your suppressed sneezing.
All life bar the physical life is conceptual or imaginary.
All living religions are a form of betrayal
All my life I have been a martyr to acute hearing.
All my life I have been struggling with my back teeth.
All my uncles were intellectuals in unfashionable cities.
All night I writhed about in agony yet again;
All one needs to know about God is that He is never in fact there.
Allow me, if I may, to take advantage of this crude instrument
Allow me, Lord, to do good – if that is what you have already
    chosen for me.
Allow me, love, to insist upon the impossible.
Allow me to tell you precisely what I tell Almighty God about you.
All poets fail. That is, perhaps, what poetry is.
All right, said God. That's enough charming, voluble Celts.
All right; we are the opposite of an island again. So what?
All Scripture is more or less fantasy, more or less
All striking features will have stories attached to them;
All talk of lovers' perfections is so much impercipience.
All talk of superhuman meaning is, in the end, fraud.
All that happened before I returned to the Church –
All that has to do with alcohol is unbearably tedious.
All these erections which the Lord God hides behind
All these guides are, it seems to me, essentially liars.
All these wits, all these truly fantastic characters,
All the thinkers I have ever met were arrogant, ignorant, shits.
All this acute discussion of highly advanced farting noises
All this insane machinery for posthumous benefit!
All those people listening intently to unintentional silences!
All those people who think they can predict the State's future
All those who have been bitten by a blind man (or woman)
All those who have greatly entertained themselves inside a church
    at dawn
All will be well, and all will be stone dead too;
All will be well – in perhaps a rather special sense of 'well'.
Almighty God does not need to grope any angelic buttocks;
Almighty God, swinging upon a non-existent rope,

Almighty God, swinging upon a thin, dangerous chain,
Almighty God, you surely must have some idea what you are doing?
Almost everybody is sinking on the wrong boat.
Almost every day that fall, I took a small tart to the attic
Almost nothing gets said. And even less gets translated.
A lot of really great cutlery is being made in Scotland these days!
A lot of this "Jewish" stuff is actually Greek, you know?
Although, as I write this, I am still laughing uncontrollably,
Although I am perhaps almost frighteningly intelligent, Rae,
Although I did not ask to be made Oblivian,
Although no-one is more sceptical in such matters than myself,
Although our forefathers (Bless them!) may have failed again and
     again
Although she died forty years ago, I still have one of her baps
Although the atheist is not necessarily a foul, imperceptive turd,
Although the likes of you would never be able to offend God,
Although we had sex daily for several decades back to back,
Always these interesting trains going in the opposite direction;
A man may smile and smile and not be a violinist at all;
A man's life is never quite over until
A man's life is not over until
A mere fifty years later, what he had said was written down.
Am I alone in detecting here a reference
A million million million very very narrow avoidances
Am I not then to be allowed to say anything about the Jews?
Am I still too young to die, I ask myself;
Am I the only person who finds the universe rather unconvincing?
A moment of hope passed; returned; then passed again;
A monk from Santa Cruz, with his large, badly tuned pipes,
A monotheistic religion with three Gods is, certainly,
A mother of five who was gazing, amazed, at her only child
An appalling pain shatters me whenever I have to lift
An awful lot more seems to have changed during the night.
An awful lot seems to have changed back during the night;
And Death shall start to fart uncontrollably.
And did those balls
And Eve said to Adam: "Have you still not finished yet?
And God said: Let there be language!
And here is the story of Belshazzar's Fast, a comparatively little-
     known tale:

And he said in a most solemn voice: "This is my bap.
And is this really the same skirt which, several decades ago,
And now, in addition, I'm falling to bits too.
And now I seem to be losing the power in my legs.
And so the two little arses proceeded on up the hill;
And the Lord said: Strive ever, cretins, to do the unavoidable.
And then, one morning, *Scheherazade*, alas, slept in.
And then, suddenly, gloriously, I finally understood
And there came a voice from Heaven which said: "Erm… One
    moment…"
And thus one generation after the next discovers
And what of the world to come after the world to come? Eh?
And when they saw the Lord shaking a mountain over their heads,
An elevator rises slowly in the hollows behind my eye
An entire country talking the wrong language?
An exciting poet? He isn't even an *unexciting* poet.
A new moon? Why? What was wrong with the old one?
Angela, if only the whole world were as delightful
A nice twang is as strong an argument for world peace
An island whose centre is nowhere and perimeter everywhere
Anna Karenina is not really all that good, is it, Nigel?
An odd building in a field, with no clear path leading to it;
A nosebleed! Sudden astonishment! As if not even the Great War
Another project is the last bloody thing I need at the moment,
    actually.
Another troubled night. This unbearable itching
An unknown man who lived well in a fine house
Any intelligent man who takes this sort of nonsense seriously
Anyone who dies with pubic hair has lived an infinitely long time;
Anyone who looks at our flag in the wrong way
Any real man whose private parts have been removed will, naturally,
Any real poet does not have favourite words.
Any scholar will routinely exaggerate his linguistic abilities.
Apart, I suppose, from the fact that nobody reads them,
A peacock ran up and down her bedroom, screaming its head off.
A people, a tribe, a family; a communal grave
A perfect man lay in great beauty before me.
A pleasant Saturday afternoon. Although that large slug
A poem is often the secretion of an unrecognised pervert.
A poem should fall down all available stairways at once

A poet can hardly afford to be without *some* favourite words.
Apparently, God cares greatly about which direction we piss in.
Apparently she thought of herself as Old English;
A remote relative of mine once heard Charles Darwin say: "This fool
Aren't children adorable? You know, I sometimes think
Are there any rooms anywhere here in which people have never
Are we still in History or not, do you think, darling?
Are we supposed to take all this seriously?
Are you by any chance in favour of world poverty? Eh?
Are you by any chance pale because you've been working too hard?
Are you really saying it is wise to shun the Gentile?
Arriving in Heaven, he found there the old air
Arriving in Heaven, he found there the old chair
Arriving in Heaven, he found there the old hair
"A royal pension"? Whenever I hear the phrase,
Arrr! It is Oi who is a-being of a-having a-done of it.
As a 55-year-old pervert with a bad heart condition,
As a figure of international unimportance,
As a first approximation, I cry out, "——"!
As a fully fledged Oblivian heterosexual failure,
As a lifelong feminist, I say this to women: "Listen.
As a man who has exploited almost every single Oblivian
As a matter of fact, no-one has ever had a previous life.
As a modest man who talks to the Transcendent every day,
As an almost perfect human being, you ask me why
As a pederast of genuinely international significance,
As a penetrator into many of the secret places
As a "person of almost unbelievable crudity",
As a proud Bolivian, I take the final, triumphant strides
As a sad git whom no-one has ever genuinely loved,
As a woman, I
As far as I can see, the mountain path is deserted;
As far as I'm aware, there is no evidence
As far as I'm concerned, you can shove your ferns
As for dying, our servants will presumably do that for us too.
As for Independence, quite frankly I object to it.
As for myself, you can see that I am finished.
As for *rigor mortis*, I suspect it too is over-rated;

As for the so-called United States of America,
A sharp wind from the Andes blows about my extended
As I am carried out head-first to where the lane meets the new
  highway,
As I improvise my way through this benign disaster,
As I sink beneath the high waves of continued English oppression,
As I sit here with an understandably superior expression,
As I sit here with steam coming out of my oppressed ears,
As it was my habit to give the Emperors useful advice,
As I was leaving *The Happy Fascist* – with mixed feelings, I hasten
  to add –
As I was waiting in solitude for my executioners,
As llama flocks climb stiff chasms, alpaca lambs lambent cliffs leap,
As, long ago, the never-yet-conquered Oblivians
A small journalist from Japan with genuinely charming genitals
A solemn face is a sacred shield for most depravities;
As one of Europe's thirteen or fourteen leading intellectuals,
As one of this country's thirty-one leading intellectuals,
As, on yet another ordinary, darkening evening,
As perhaps the most culturally diverse region of all Europe,
As regards my religion, darling, you are sitting on it.
As she shoved the warm, delicate meringue shyly into my face,
As someone famously sensitive to *nuance*, Pontius,
As someone who has been a World Cup finalist,
As someone who has more than once been stuck to this very floor,
As someone who has (twice!) been called "almost heart-breakingly
  attractive",
As so often happens here in Oblivia
As the best friend of at least a third of the Trinity,
As the greatest writer of perhaps the last five thousand years,
As the great Hillel said: "The more women there are,
As the Great Wall of the World's Indifference
As the old priest pulled two strings in the confessional box,
As "the perfect man" he was, one assumes, impotent.
As the priests ran up and down, shrieking with fear,
As the rain pours down on the street, the light at the window
As the Romans might say: All roads lead to Scunthorpe.
As the son and heir of a none-too-successful provincial shopkeeper,
As the train was about to enter Dorgonovastes Station,
As they stood at all the windows, looking out towards Russia,

9

As to how millions of bad angels could suddenly emerge
Astonishing fate! Quite surrounded by idiots,
As to what might happen to you after you have ceased to exist,
As to whether, Les, all three members of the Trinity
As to which of the great religions is, downright, the stupidest,
As to which particular Catholic youth it was who first seduced
    Oscar Wilde,
As to why I keep a harp beneath my bed, Doreen,
As to why the occasional small neat incision
A strange, exotic wayside memorial to a dog (or cat?)
A strangely erotic wayside Crucifixion
A sudden, stabbing pain at the end of my nose
As you stood at the window, looking out towards Rutherglen,
As you stood at the window, looking towards Rurrenabaque,
A systematic onslaught on all that is good and pure
At a recent *Exhibition of Heterosexual Teenage Calligraphy*
At first, in the beginning, there was no such thing as Time.
A thing of beauty can sometimes get royally on one's gonads;
At his coronation, the King took a white mare
At last, after several thousand billion years of oppression,
At last! A group of female agnostics have climbed Everest!
At last, I have found something I am happy to call 'God'.
At last I realised I was alone. Utterly alone.
At least I have the immense satisfaction of knowing
At least our pottery was not the pornographic sort
At length one begins to suspect how little most authority figures
    know.
At length one begins to suspect how little most writers know too.
At midnight, admiring the stars, waiting, slowly dampening
At night, by the wild, desolate shore of San Francisco,
At ninety-three, more or less, I gave her her first orgasm.
At ninety-three, more or less, I gave her her second orgasm.
At ninety-two, he was buried with full military honours,
A true angel would *never* piss in anyone's coffee *even once*.
A true Holy of Holies should always be empty.
A true poet, like Blod, always has much better things to do
At some point in his or her life, every father has to ask themselves
At some point, it will be discovered that I have always been a
    classic.
At ten to six in the evening, if my old watch is still accurate,

At the age of sixty-two, I suddenly realised
At the end, he was up on his pole, farting uncontrollably.
At the Estación Central, at about five past eleven,
At the Last Judgement, a sort of transcendental stink
At the marriage feast, they had reached the crude animal noises
    stage;
At the moment, my ambition, more than anything else,
Attributing one's own writings to a superhuman agency
Au fond, who does not wish to pull down the Lady Fortune's
    drawers?
Autumn rainfall, by the look of it. Autumn, certainly.
A vast crowd often stood here, shrieking obscenities,
A very simple solution immediately suggests itself, Vince.
A wall and, among many leaves, a strange flattened dome
A wise and delightful old priest, increasingly troubled by his syphilis,
A woman was running to a bus-stop, carrying a long wooden
    snake,
A woman will often have to stick her backside up into the air

"Base coward!" he said, and pointed towards the sea.
Basically, by "the Muse" we mean "c——", do we not?
Basically, my life is over – in the sense that
Bavaria! Surely a certain magical echo
Because it is profoundly inconvenient
Because of my sensational abilities, Maurice,
Because some bloody chemical found some half-arsed way of
    repeating itself,
Beckett! Your complete failure to solve the Irish problem
Before all these things started to go wrong with me
Before even Oblivia was, I am
Before things started to go badly wrong with me
Be good, and God will give you a *fantastic* reward!
Being out of one's mind is the ultimate spiritual experience.
Believe me, I am not afraid of using either of the N-words.
Believe me, Madam, if it were not for your tattoo,
Believe me, my dear, if all women were like you,
Believe nothing anyone tells you about their sexual lives.
Believe, oh Bolivia, my invaluable, oblivious beloved,

Beloved Madonna, whose sad buttocks in the dawn
Beloved Roseangle, where I left that superb carpet,
"Bend over!" shrieked the nun to the simpering dancer,
Beneath the ancient lintels, I once again start up a fire.
Beneath what one would like to call your star-filled eras,
Be sure of it. In Largs we shall meet again
Be thou unreal, even as thy God is unreal;
Better gaga with God, Stan, than sane with Satan;
Better one single, beautiful, plagiarised epigram
Between the Great Book and the various collections of fairy tales
Be very careful. For one thing, I am a war criminal.
Beyond all this, the intense desire to be surrounded by many
    thousands of admiring Bolivians.
Beyond the ridges, the towns, so brilliantly lit
Big, brawny man, remember, hard at hammering
Birds of Oblivia! I
Birth is, essentially, an act of aggression
Blake, who preferred his visions to limitless but tedious truth,
Blowing people up has never been one of my mainstream religious
    projects.
Bolivia, China – and (just possibly) ancient Greece –
Bolivia has survived! (Hasn't it?)
Bolivia! Home of many ancient civilisations!
Bolivia! Peerless land of mountains and floods!
Bolivia! Sad relic of departed worth!
Bolivia unimportant? What! Our infinite, multiform
Bolivia! Whom once the whole of South America
Bradley! Unless (very broadly)
Brasil! Like an immense, fat husband, your crushing weight
Bravely he refused to shake hands with his executioner;
Breasts are, if nothing else, a magnificent riposte
Breasts don't seem to influence the sun all that much;
Breathes there a man who would merely fart uncontrollably
Breathes there the Oblivian, with soul so dead,
Buñuel! The sort of person who shits in front of mirrors
Burton! Words fail me! (Which is not entirely inappropriate.)
But –
But all that happened before I became a Christian.
But for a certain difficulty in staying alive,
But for her large witch's hat, the retired Senior Civil Servant

But for the bells, this place would now be wonderfully quiet;
But for the kindness of imaginary people,
But for the multiple hernia, I trust my erotic technique
But I thought you said you worshipped my toes!
But most people are incompetent! Have you not grasped that yet?
But where would the challenge have been for Perfection to create
    a perfect universe?
But why must there be any recompense for this?
By a "magnificent figure" is usually meant
By and large, I have kept myself clear of vicious and disgusting habits;
By *Mühltal*, on a sudden slope of ground,
By now, I am tired of asking people to marry me.
By now, I have already outlived so many successful people;
By now I have outlived some mighty shits indeed;
By now I have won a few (fairly minor) prizes for potency.
By the edge of the sea, at night, a proud young Oblivian
By the rivers of Babylon we started to fart uncontrollably;
By the time the sun rose again, I had fallen off the shelf.
By the way, it's a quotation from Robert Burns:
"By the way, there's a lunatic in the next room."

Caledonia! Why not try getting up off your arse?
Calling Virginia Woolf "a poof" seems, somehow,
Calmly the sacred poet asserts the completely impossible;
Canada! If I may say so, the rampant degeneracy
Can I possibly be the only one to have noticed
Can I really have become a complete sexual superfluity?
Can it be raining on this river all the way to Riberalta?
Can one be forcibly converted to the true religion?
Catholics – or, indeed, believers in magic in general –
Cease, dear friend, to explore my private parts;
Celts are rightly celebrated for the neatness of their whorls.
Certain fatal ailments are, alas, inherently ridiculous.
Certainly, God can work rather well as a cartoon character;
Certainly it was an extremely well-timed death
Certainly, to be led astray by a light from Heaven
Charismatic ancient lunatics, who were wrong about nearly
    everything,

Children! Ah! Bless them!

Children? Yes; yes. In general, one sees the point –

Chocolate and gullibility are our richest native fruits.

Chocolate, fruit-flavoured water, cheese, mildly pornographic films,

"Christ!" cried out have near not of ten enough I (aye!)

Christ crumbled into the dust much like everyone else.

Christianity too is, basically, a rip-off from the Jews.

Christian passer-by! Yes, you! Stop doing that at once!

Christmas again! Come here, dear. Now. Pull this as hard as you can.

Christmas again! So. Are you wearing it or not?

Christ (who in many ways was extremely Oblivian)

Clanking arrogantly into the sacred bog,

Clearly, my heart is just about to succumb

Clearly, not enough poems have been written about how bridges

Clearly, not enough poems have been written about how rooms

Clearly, not enough poems have been written about how my underwear

Clearly, there was nothing wrong with Queen Victoria's reproductive equipment.

Clearly you have forgotten how I used to wipe you clean

Cold in the fridge, with cheeses piled above it,

Come all ye atheistical old nancy-boys of France,

Come down, you stupid old fool, from the top of the antiques cabinet!

Come, Jesu – with thy thicked-gigantic thews

Come let me clamber (O gain, ah, gain!) onto hot Christ's kinglike corpse;

Come to my arms, you half-witted old pervert!

Comparatively few people would like to have electronic wires

Compared to me, Juno, nobody is the real thing.

Compatriots! Alas, your legendary beauty must attract

Compatriots! When last you met, a distant crack

Compatriots who have with O'Kupczyk bled!

Concerning the Jews, the Scots, and other such vagabonds,

Confused, we ignored the Man of God who was having sex in the cupboard.

Confused, we ignored the Men of God who were making love in the kitchen.

Congratulate me! I have become a virgin again.
Consider, Gertrude. You are not your brother. Are you?
Considering how ill I must be, I feel surprisingly good;
Considering that he never knew the language
Contempt! O second most liberating of emotions!
Convicted of sodomy halfway down a coalmine,
Copulation, I suspect, is falling right out of fashion nowadays.
Could everything not in fact be something else?
Could Leonardo too somehow have been (at least partly) Oblivian?
Couldn't you do something about this problem, O Lord?
Couldn't you love me for my physical shortcomings, Deirdre?
Could there be anything more absurd than the present
"Courage!" he said, and ran like f——k for the door.
"Coward!" he said, and pointed toward the seat.
Cowards and fools! I know that my own resistance to torture
Cragged even-ing peaks, streak ragged clouds; did Jesus (calm!) the
  Christ
Creeping through the intense, nocturnal silence
Cretin, who gloriously ended up in the wrong continent entirely!
Crossing into Oblivia, I think: Thank God, at long last –
Crossing the famous battlefield, well, we had a bit of an argument.
——! But, no – I won't misuse that word of all our words.

Dagmar, there is something I can no longer quite keep from you.
Daniel, as the third lion ripped off his other arm,
Dante, that great master of the verbal three-card-trick,
Darling, although I have an almost unique musculature,
Darling, but for your indecencies with other men,
Darling, don't be so proud of those five or six fine eyes
Darling, have I not already often enough probed
Darling, have I not proved often enough already
Darling, I'm afraid your almost unbelievable stupidity
Darling – I *never* called you an absolute shit!
Darling, just because I may once have hit your father,
Darling, just because I tied up your mother once or twice,
Darling, just because your grandparents only with difficulty escaped
Darling, let me count thy breasts. One. Two. Fantastic!
Darling, let's be honest. You have become fat and unattractive.

Darling, please open the door just a little bit wider. You know?

Darling, there is something which I ought perhaps to have told you before.

Darling, to urinate into a new washing-machine is perhaps

Darling, when you told me you loved me "in a non-physical way",

Darwin! Poof!

Dawn at long last! Now may those magic powers

Dawn came and went, but Leonora remained asleep.

Day after day, nothing. Absolutely nothing.

Dear Cardinal – as one pervert to another –

Dear force, in which for years we used to smell

Dear Friend! A few malicious charges of gross indecency

Dear friend, not even thirty-five years of incarceration

Dear friend – or perhaps I should say: dear former friend –

Dear friend, those so-called critics who said your latest book

Dear friend: Your second son looks quite astonishingly like you!

Dear friend! Your own version of the *King Lear* story will surely

Dear Friend! You worshipped youthful energy

"Dear God, I'm bored!" said the figure on the post.

"Dear God, I'm bored!" said the figure on the tree.

Dear God, please kill a few thousand people more

Dear God – since, after all, you caused these deaths in the first place –

Dear God! To be Shakespeare's son! It is little wonder

Dear God, you have so clearly made a mess of it

Dear Homeland! Favoured child of God himself!

Dear Homeland! It grieves me much that I cannot die for you!
   [And even more that *certain other people* cannot die for you!]

Dear Homeland! It grieves me much that I cannot die for you.
   [But, alas, inescapable commitments in the South of France]

Dear Homeland! No, never shall the envious foreigner

Dear Homeland! The amazed world looks on with bated breath,

Dear Homeland! Though foreign fools talk of a "cult of leisure"

Dear Jesus, who (in a sense) loved to walk these Bolivian pathways,

Dear Mither of God, don't ever abandon me!

Dear Paul, I am very sorry to have been a prominent Nazi.

Dear retired, adored little private opening,

Dear Sirs, when I turned down contemptuously that pension you offered me last year,

Death is even more unlike a transient vapour

Death is something like farting, perhaps taken to extremes;
Death, I would advise you not to lose your sense of honour.
Death, I would advise you not to lose your sense of humour.
Deep down, all parables and allegories must be false.
Deep down, men don't know nearly as much as women do.
Deep down, we know we have nothing to do with our parents'
    private parts.
Deep down, women know three-quarters as much as men do.
Deeply upset by the loss of my mother's fine old drawers,
Delightful flowers, we must laugh uncontrollably
Diana! You seem to be doing extremely well for yourself
Dickens was, in many ways, a bit of a prat.
Did Burns or Scott have the bigger penis, would you suppose?
Did I perhaps say unforgivable things last night?
Did you notice what an absolutely amazing colour
Did you see that tall nun laughing at the Pope's funeral?
Did you touch me then? Or was that somebody else?
Die ganze Sache ist eine andere Welt!
Discovering one's true sexuality at the age of forty-five,
Discovering one's true sexuality at the age of forty-six,
Discovering one's true sexuality at the age of ninety-seven,
Doctor! Friends! Lovers! Husbands! Sisters! Cousins!
Does anyone shit in Shakespeare? One assumes somebody must.
Does every man, I wonder, feel like this at ninety-nine?
Does it matter all that much if I am slowly going mad?
Does language tell us, Angel, what we tell it to tell us?
Does the truth hate you? If so, the feeling is clearly mutual.
Dogs die, and that's it. Where does all that love go to?
Dogs that are dead and buried do often love to bark;
Do I deserve this almost terrifying level of success?
Do I now regret the almost seven thousand days spent in pubs?
Do not call him "a long-dead Jew", merely because
Do not call it 'murder' merely because
Do not dare to say, dear one, that I know nothing of the world;
Do not force me, O great libraries, to break in through the
    windows
Do not forget my eyes
Do not forget that my eyes
Do not go farting uncontrollably, dear, into that good night.
Do not go gentle into that enormous acid vat.

Do not just pretend to be an Oblivian!
Don Quixote is not really all that good, is it?
Don't blame yourself, silly woman, for finding me irresistible;
Don't bother reading any of my poetry. No. Really.
Don't call us stone-worshippers, merely because
Don't flaunt your genitals like that. Good night!
Don't let them ever guess you worship the sort of thing
Don't look now – but there's a bird standing on your shoulder.
Don't tell me any more about the great poetry you are 'going to
     write'.
Don't tell me I've disappointed yet another woman!
Don't weep for Adonais. That sad fruit
Don't you agree that you are really a very nice person?
Doris, there is something I can no longer keep from you.
Doug, do not do the deed thou most would dig;
Down by the salley gardens, I started to fart uncontrollably.
Downhill all the way for centuries since Bannockburn?
"Do you find me intriguing?" "No. Not in the slightest,"
Do you happen to know the proper name for this part of my body?
Do you have to say *quite* so much about their rear ends?
Do you hear the little girls snoring, oh my brothers of the faith?
Do you know if you often sleep with your legs
Do you not fade and return, like light or music?
Do you really not have to decide to rejoin the world?
Do you really want to know what I did with your last present?
Do you remember how once, Diana, you called me a dirty old perve?
Do you think your grandmothers, or your great-grandmothers,
Do you too think of yourself as a pornographer as such?
Do you wish to know who I learned my immense compassion from?
Do you wonder why I kneed the Headmaster in the groin
Dread force, which made both my wife's nostrils and the Cairngorms!
Drench us, sweet love, from sky (O! white!), O ghostly whole;
Drinking contraband Ribena in Riberalta,
Drinking dry wine for twelve years by the shores of Titicaca,
Drinking to the dregs the bitter wine of popularity,
Dying at last! Thank God! Yes! Dying at last!
Dying in childbirth? I mean to say. Where's the morality in that?

Effete fools! I at least am standing up to be counted!
1825! Most glorious of years!
1827! Most glorious of years!
1826! Second most glorious of years!
Eight shots fired over the grave of an alcoholic pederast
Emotion falsified in recollection
"END EVIL" said the sign hanging outside the small church;
England is, perhaps, a little too much with us.
English must be the world's most bloody awful language
Epidemics, enslavement, embarrassment, embassies,
"Er," said God. "I may just have done something completely
    unforgivable there."
Escaping by a side-door, the Inca fell into the river.
Eternity is talking to me, Trev.
Eternity is whispering secrets to me again.
Euphemisms for drunkenness are even more numerous
Europe! Sad, old continent of perverts, grief and ruins!
Evadne, I had expected so, so much better.
Even about their own lives people know virtually nothing.
Even after the body had been more or less brought
Even as an extremely old man, my son
Even a very stupid person like you must surely realise
Even a whimper of ignorance can be lethal
Even for the emotionalists who worship their own instincts
Evening. A solitary agricultural worker
Evening. The parks are quiet, except where the soldiers
Even Lenzie can have little to show more beautiful
Even nuns can kill? So what? This in no way affects
Even on the newest islands they believe the same old rubbish
Even our llamas are flamboyantly heterosexual.
Even the calm seas can and will lap Oblivia,
Even the way, O Stalin, in which you stained your underpants
Even the way she sat was not that of a mere mortal,
Even though the last Pope was an absolute martyr to piles,
Even though we had been expecting this terrible news,
Even though you have always told me you feel no affection for me,
Even to me my own early years seem particularly impossible;
Even to someone who knows he is always dealing with cretins
Eventually, the world will apologise to my homeland.
Even when they are used to forestall fatal infections

Even young girls can tell that deliberate silence
Every bloody week, this intrusion in my head
Everybody suddenly burst out farting uncontrollably.
Every day, in the rarely visited Art Gallery,
Every morning, I get up from my bed and cry out
Every nation has the coastline it deserves, Lavinia.
Everyone brings up children in completely the wrong way.
Everyone else is real as you are yourself, Orlando.
Everyone here has already forgotten you completely, my dear
     friend.
Everyone is already living in harmony with Nature;
Every remark which assumes the existence of God
Every single one of us has given birth to a monster.
Every so often I quiver at the thought of how brilliant
Every so often, one sees a wall behind which one would like to live.
Everything about the earth looks interesting in moonlight.
Everything about this new Pontiff seems to whisper: "Pervert!"
Everything except the earth looks interesting in moonlight.
Everything God does is an insult against God.
Everything is somewhere in the long queue for oblivion.
Everything I touch is turning to gold! Well – not *real* gold,
Everything, no matter how boring, is completely unrepeatable.
Everything seems to be falling to bits. (Trust God!)
Everything to do with 'recreational drugs' is tedious.
Everything you could possibly need is here in this book.
Every time you look, something has been changed for the worse.
Everywhere, of course, must have come from somewhere else.
Evidently being astonishingly wonderful is not enough;
Exactly how many neighbouring cultures do you wish to ruin?
Exactly what we need. Long, long poems about plants!
Excited by Master Eckhart, I began to quiver uncontrollably.
Excuse me, darling, while I run a mile or so sharpish.
Excuse me, dear – but why do your ears smell of toothpaste?
Excuse me, Madam. Do you know where you've put your finger?
Excuse me, Lord. That happens to be my daughter's box.
Existence couldn't be added to a nicer non-person
Existence is, basically, for slipping in and out of, unnoticed.
Existence is not a clear sign upon a wall.
Experience is the name we all give to our private parts.
Experience, like a deaf musician, tries not to weep

Expose me at once, Vince, to the full glory of your trembling heart.

Faced with a genuinely interesting bit of schist,
Facts are wonderful, no doubt. And yet, surely I too
'Failure' hardly seems quite an adequate word
Faint rainbows throughout the city all night
Faith is, above all else, a somewhat dishonest form
Faking the evidence is a perfectly normal occurrence
Farewell then, to all our ancient Bolivian fame!
Fat, impotent oaf! Your most puzzling longevity
Fearful that the devout might possibly try to kill him,
Fellow citizens, who can lie, f—— and drive a car (even if not
    quite simultaneously),
Few of us are quite at our best while excreting waste;
Few of us, I suspect, would *choose* to be a tapeworm, no matter
    how long
Few saints, I suspect, are terribly understanding people.
Few things, surely, are much less interesting than prostitution.
Few would believe, looking at the map of Oblivia,
Few works are so vulnerable to out-of-context selection
Fifty years after his death, it was still an Age of Ignorance.
Firm and erect the *Proud Bolivian* stood:
First, a few words about the seven different types of soul.
First, a few words about the History Professor's nipples.
First eyes – then, if fortunate, telephone numbers;
Firstly, let me say something, Madam, about your hidden scar.
First of all, Horace, take both your buttocks in your hands,
First of all, I would just like to thank Almighty God
First there is something I must say about these chains.
First was the world much as a great anus made,
Five of my nine favourite writers were left-handed!
Five of my nineteen favourite thinkers have (or had) tits!
Five of my ninety favourite human beings were white men!
Five thousand years later, all that was left was a large stain
Flicking through my tax-forms in a dentist's waiting-room,
Flodden? No, sorry. Never heard of it. But my wife
Fool! None of my houses owes a thing to the slavery of the
    peasants.

Fool! We answer your question thus: Shut up right now!
Football is all right for perverts, I suppose.
For all of us, there will come a final blow-out;
For a long time, I admit, I thought you were off your head.
For a long time I have been staring, profoundly amazed,
For a long time it was not noticed that the universe was expanding.
For a long time now, I have gone to bed with no clothes on.
For a man of the cloth, his collection of little knickers
For a moment, I thought they must have recognised me!
For a thorough-going idealist philosopher to catch syphilis
For a while I was very angry with my best friend's second wife.
Forced to survive in an attic for years, with one's head stuck in a
    toilet-bowl,
For centuries the tasselled feet raced along these roads.
Forgive me, my angel, if I too crudely pulled out
For God's sake, Clarinda, at least let me see your pouter.
For God's sake, keep the people safe in Oblivia!
For heaven's sake, what else could I possibly have said?
For many years I thought the other sex peed out of their navels.
For many years I was the second greatest idiot on earth.
For me, there is something almost unbearably exciting
For me, there is something unbearably tedious
For me, the sight of a malicious academic sunbathing
For me, the sound of a sarcastic secretary moaning
For more or less the third time in my life
For my favourite rule of thumb theory about the higher life
For only the second time in my life
For some deep, mystical reason, I have always liked the name Fanny.
For some reason, Bach played by women with no hands (eh?)
For the first time in my life
For the first time in years, I looked closely at my penis this morning.
For the foreigner who dares laugh at us, only one answer
For the moment our legends have stalled. We don't want another
    argument.
Fortunately, I had no faith in Ibrian justice even to begin with.
For twenty years, those grim, aggressive accents
Forty years waiting at a bathroom door, Ignacio,
For weeks, that portable toilet just across the road
For years, I have gone to bed wearing an amateurish toga.
For years I have worshipped that which hangs down at the front

For years in these buildings – this very room. Or for a night –
Four or five times the old man groaned and eructated;
Frae this dey oan ah pronounce ye fushers oav maws.
Frankly, Adam, your crude and overbearing heterosexuality
Frankly, I could do with having a lot fewer ideas.
Frankly, I doubt if Jesus was much good as a dinner companion.
Frankly, I'd prefer a God who let you take the piss a bit more
Frankly, it is just not the sort of thing that God would say, is it?
Frankly, Madam, your fondness for sexual cruelty
Frankly, said God; by now I'm a little bit disenchanted.
Friend! Having now read your matchless *Dithyrambs frae the
    Dowanhill Deedle Doddle,*
Friends, if our Church is not the Everlasting Wound
Friends, when I am dead, bring nine pairs of common or garden
    knickers,
Friend! To call someone's *Autobiography* "seriously under-
    researched"
Friend, your bizarre combination of cynicism and fertility worship
Friend, your magnificent poem about having sex with the dead
From castle to castle wandered the old Oblivian troubador,
From her hands I received favours which seemed to baffle
    description –
From the most civilised town in all the Americas,
From the rich store of my as yet unpublished poems,
From the sky, there descended an extremely effete voice, saying:
From time to time, of course, I wonder what happened;
F——k! My foot is caught in a trap and I can't get it out!
F——k off! And this time take your dead friend with you.
F——k off, Imperialist! We can work these machines ourselves now.
"F——!" said the old priest – somewhat to our surprise –
Fujiyama! Compared to Mount Chachacomani,

Gabbro (a coarsely crystalline igneous rock, composed
Gadlinium – a rare earth metal with the chemical symbol, Gd –
Galeopithecus, the so-called 'flying lemur',
Galipot, the turpentine which exudes from the cluster-pine,
Gallium – which has the atomic number 31 –
Gamboge, a yellow gum-resin, which is chiefly extracted

Gannister, a hard, close-grained, siliceous stone
Ganzid! Precarious homeland of perhaps my favourite ancestor!
Genghis Khan himself (greatest of all the Chinese leaders)
Gerard! Do please tell us even more about Jesus Christ!
Giacomo Antonio Domenico Michele Maria Puccini! Poof!
Give it up, Mate! You simply cannot write!
Give me the wherewithal to pass your severest tests, O Lord!
Given that it was a complete disaster, I thought it went strangely well.
Given that your father was an alcoholic wastrel,
Giving money to priests will help you get into Heaven.
Gladly do I, good God, bare on myself the blame
Glory be to God for all being – but for the bad bits –
Go and see which of the poets is at the door tonight.
God, all those halfwits who imagined those that they loved,
God – a much neater term than auto-hypnosis –
God could not be everywhere – so He invented child molesters? –
God created everything – but not the Devil. Obviously.
God forbid that Scriptures should be translated accurately!
God has more to worry about than the size of your credentials.
God, how much I dislike having to talk to my neighbours!
God, I am what you made me. Why couldn't you have left me alone?
God, if there were a special prize for sheer lack of talent,
God, I hate these people! (Who are they, by the way?)
God, I'm depressed. And yet,
God is also the worst nonsense we can think.
God is a selection of impressive verbal effects;
God is a sort of feeling one has when well up in the mountains;
God is certainly not an essential problem of Life.
God is giggling more or less all the time.
God is Nature's sole mistake.
God is the highest rubbish we can talk.
God never renders us senseless for no good reason.
God punishes us for being what he made us. No?
God seems to be a shorthand term for certain effects in the head.
God, since he is not there, can hardly be crushed, can he?
God's is the crime; and ours is the punishment.
Gods nearly always think they are more powerful than they are.
God, there is something I (most humbly) want to tell you.
God tries his best to hide. But his large protruding ears
God, what boring women

God, who has seventeen legs and three weak eyes,
Goethe's *Faust* is not really all that good, is it, Ute?
Good Friday. Alas, I find I have slept in after all.
Good God! All the people here are still alive!
Good God – do I have to do everything myself?
Good God, yes; that girl certainly did know how to
Good Heavens! I have now outlived Bolivar!
Good Heavens! I have now outlived Napoleon!
Good Heavens! I have outlived even Bertie Russell by now!
Good news, Sir! There are now no fleabites on your wife's buttocks;
Good news! The whole place is now jumping with religious maniacs!
Go on then. Ask me anything you want.
Go on then! Quote another one out of context.
Gossip is so much more entertaining than most art, isn't it?
Great Compatriot – who certainly did not die of syphilis!
Great Compatriot, who so nearly invented photography!
Great experts – such as can tell the Incas from the Aztecs –
Great land of manipulative, warm-hearted drunks!
Great leader! – who murdered virtually no-one!
Gringo, it seems, is a term of Scotch derivation.
Gross, talentless turd! But, no: let us not descend to mere verbal
   abuse.

Ha, ha, ha, ha! Wobble, wobble, wobble, wobble! Bang! Oops.
   What?
Had it not been for his essentially erotic conception of suicide,
Had the enemy commander not fallen into a hole,
Hail, Youth! I tremble
Ha! I still remember finding him trussed up out on the balcony
Half a million condoms is probably enough
Halfway up the mountain, I wondered: What's that strange smell?
Hanging in the *Sexual Institute* in Berlin
Hardly matters. What does matter is this.
Has any great philosopher ever really drowned in Lake Titicaca?
Ha! The suave, impressive way in which you pursued those islands
Have I been kidnapped and brought here to this garage?
Have I done anything else but make mistakes?
Have I landed you in it? Please say, no.

"Have I not told you before that I am gay?" asked Jovah.
Have I really had to live in this dreadful dump all my life?
Have I told you already where the cosmos will disappear to?
Have you quite finished? Don't let me interrupt you.
Have you taken leave of your bloody senses, Admiral?
Have you written epigrams on every chair in this flat?
Having all my life occupied an imaginary tenancy,
Having crawled off into the undergrowth to wait for death,
Having hidden for several hours underneath the bed of the King,
Having hidden for several minutes under the King's cloak,
Having hidden for several seconds right underneath the King,
Having invaded the Palace and pissed all over the furniture,
Having lived in various embassy cupboards for twenty years or so,
Having made the world out of nothing, a sudden doubt
Having managed to get so many things completely wrong,
Having no insight whatsoever, Maximus became a political
    commentator;
Having nothing in particular to say, Magnus became a cultural
    commentator;
Having somehow managed to latch onto a source of superhuman
    wisdom,
Hearing someone fall off the small table in the next room,
He began to play the maracas, but was hit on the head
He "discovered the truth about the world", did he? How
    frightfully vulgar!
He does not die who merely ceases to exist;
He fell forward, dead. Or he might as well have done.
He gave a huge yawn and his latest wig fell off;
Heidegger once, having farted with immense *brio* in class,
Heine – another love poet who died of syphilis –
He is, in fact, a member of the middle classes;
He lived in the full light of history for forty (some say sixty) years.
Hell is a woman angrily refusing to pretend
Hell is the invention of emotional children.
Hello. I'm in utter torment.
"Hello, little girl!" said the wolf. "Is that a shotgun I see?"
Hello. My life is over and I have failed
"Hello, Sister! Hello, Sister! Hello, Sister!
Hello there. Do I exist?
Hello there. I am floating ambiguously between

Hello there. I'm past it.
Hello there, my proud young beauty! Are those muscles your own?
Hello. Three people lying in a single bed –
Hello. You don't know who I am, do you?
Hello. Your mother was a prostitute, by the way.
He loved the non-Existent to excess.
Help! Help! We are trapped! Let us out into the air!
Here. Count your own bloody slaves before you talk about ours.
Here even the alcoholics, as they fall with a rare grace
Here, in a large box burning at the edge of the small lake,
Here in the far north, about Lake Huiñamarca
Here is some of what we can say about the Unknowable:
'Here lies a great friend of mine, who was once very active sexually.
Here lies a pederastic Man of God.
Here, likewise, is the story of Belshazzar's Fart.
Here no Oblivian can pass uninterested.
Here! This place is full of pictures of naked women!
Here we have a photograph of me meeting God. Nice, eh?
He took a long path through the woods and never came back.
He was hit by a huge yam which fell off the wall
He was hit on the head, fatally, while playing the pan-pipes,
He who does not hate his father and mother
He who genuinely admires women will suffer for it.
Hidden near the wall, a giant stone vagina
Higher than lakes, clouds, jets, and whatever next,
His bold, unswerving faith that Telboig was not ouvangirate
His brave, unswerving faith that Telboig *was* ouvangirate
His great hatred of all abstractions – except God –
His last words were: *Don't move. Just stay like that.*
His last words were: *That machine is as lovely as ever.*
His mission in life is to smash up awkward artefacts
History comes just before "Hi there!"   .
History is a dying man with an oddly powerful erection.
History will piss in our faces too, as usual.
Hi there! Why not call me the non-Professor?
Hmm. Well. Now you come to mention it, darling,
Homosexuality is for me, above all else, a superb allegory
Hope is the Chief Inca with feathers in his hat
Ho! Take me behind the wall, kind Sir, and gaily prong me there!
How am I to exist, if, exiled from Oblivia,

How are so many people completely able to do without me?
How astonishingly distant those trees just over there are.
How, beneath what I would like to call your star-filled ears,
How can an honest person not love and venerate Oblivia?
How can Bolivia ever lose in a fair fight?
How can I be dying? I am not a weirdo. Am I?
"How can you eat this crap?" she asked;
How can you say I hate men just because I hate you?
How complex and wonderful our civilisation is!
How could I be a racist? I am of Oblivian descent.
How could I have failed to see that you are an absolute shit?
How could I have thought it mattered in the slightest
How could I possibly have known that you were mad?
How could I possibly have told you about it before?
How could I possibly have written so many poems
How could such old-fashioned weapons really kill anyone?
How dare so many women be uninterested in me?
How disconcertingly physical the real world is, Dick.
How do I love you? Let me count these notes.
How else is this bloody place to be governed at all,
How evening, like a refrigerator which a half-dead rabbi
How evening, like a refrigerator wherein half a dead rabbit
How everything you touch seems to have so much life in it!
How exciting it is to learn that your great-great-grandfather
How fortunate that the Universe as such never needs to micturate.
How good God might be is, ultimately, beside the point.
How gorgeous the earth looks in its little pink underpants!
How gratefully I now relive that morning in your office.
How greatly I now regret not mounting you in your office,
How his God nearly always lessens a human being!
How human beings do so love to flatter themselves!
How I love the mere awkwardness of their continuing existence;
How it all give to God who it hath any gate
How I wish, O My Country, I could pay you more in taxes;
How, like a bad-tempered ballet dancer wearing only one sock,
How lovely you looked, with that appallingly crude object stuck
    between your lips!
How ludicrous the sea is once again.
How many great philosophers have ever fallen into the Clyde?
How many millions have made a living from the otherworldly?

How many of us realise how ridiculous we look
How many people have been enslaved in all our histories?
How many will manage, I wonder, to make a living from me?
How many writers are involved
How much energy I have expended in going nowhere!
How much I love switching your light on and off;
How much is that dog-faced widow in the window?
How much love they had for completely unreal things!
How much, O Sweden, I envy you your reflexive pronouns!
How oddly plain the great pornographer's daughter looked
How odd that the whole Mediterranean should end, particularly,
    here.
How odd to think that, a thousand years ago now,
How odd to think that, five thousand years ago,
How odd to think that, four thousand years ago,
How odd to think that, three thousand years ago,
How odd to think that, two thousand years ago,
How often has the morning sun lovingly caressed
How on earth am I supposed to keep my hands off my doctor's bust?
How pleasant to sit in the pews again, after a decent ——,
How profoundly I worship you, oh walls of my homeland!
How reassuring that all those people are dead,
How reliable is anyone's view of their own history?
How ridiculous most of these foreign languages are.
How sad that a well-meaning attempt to address some Indian girls
How tedious Death is. Death, and his sister, History.
How the train one is travelling on oneself always seems so much
    more real
How well I recall, darling, your disconcerting suggestion
How we undervalue all earlier anxieties.
How wonderful it is to be somebody else!
How wonderful it would have been if only she had lived here!
How wonderful to walk through Lanark in the strange mist
Hmm. The Bolivian sea is particularly calm tonight.
Hmm. The Oblivian sea is peculiarly calm tonight.
Hmm. You don't suppose the universe might be upside-down, do
    you, Ella?
Huh. The Romans. Couldn't even invent Nothing.
Hullo. I am not dead yet.
Hullo. I appear to be in a world of light.

Hullo. I would like to set fire to all your future underwear.
Human life is a rehearsal for nothing.
Hullo, Love. Oh, sorry. My mistake.
Human sacrifice has certainly not yet died out, has it?
Human sacrifice is of course central to Christianity;
Human sacrifice one always tends to interpret as a failure.
Hurry back, Pervert, to your absurdly shaped country
Hurrying late last night out of the *Rat and Bondage Fetishist*,
"Hypocrisy?" Whenever I hear the word – not that I often do –

I absolutely deny that I am in fact a woman
I accuse the universe of being a severe disappointment to me.
I admired thee across the kitchen table, as thou didst disembowel
I admit that certain kinds of male authority
I adore solitude – and so I think do all my friends.
I agree that there is indeed something fishy about Chirst.
I agree that the sun is more than somewhat tedious.
I also dreamt I could hear your Dad's voice whispering to me;
I always failed to praise Eve's navel in quite the right terms.
I always kept waiting for them to do it again;
I always knew we'd get back together again.
I always thought it was a sign of love
I am absolutely outraged
I am against slavery. Very much so, in fact.
I am almost certain I heard the parrot say "F——!"
I am almost certain that the bodies on the steps of the Presidential
    Palace
I am already back in Oblivia.
I am already in Oblivia.
I am already in Oblivia again.
I am an Oblivian woman. Above all else I wish
I am a Northern barbarian. (Isn't it obvious?)
I am a very strict Calvinist, except for one particular tenet.
I am awestruck by your genius, Jim.
I am a woman. Listen to me. This is what I want.
I am bent – at least in the sense that
I am – but who gives a monkey's truss what I am? –
I am deeply grateful to the innumerable unknown copulators

I am determined to live for poetry. Er – no, sorry: for money.
I am drunk, drunk on the heady wine of undeserved success.
I am edging slowly but surely towards the firm opinion
I am essentially a religious poet, Ray.
I am excited almost to ecstasy when I think
I am excited more or less beyond endurance
I am fighting a rearguard action for what could be called fried eggs.
I am going to have to do something about probability.
I am going to have to make a careful decision here.
I am haunted by the fear that my enemies have still not suffered
  enough.
I am having problems with – well, with everything, basically.
I am, in a sense, completely honest.
I am in immense pain. And not just existentially.
I am just about to do something which
I am more and more inclining towards the perhaps bizarre view
I am more tired than any human being
I am nearly as big a criminal, Lord, as Thou art.
I am no longer capable of those acts which, above all others,
I am no longer greatly interested in what nurses wish
I am nothing – and the rest are even less.
I am not interested in what women do with other men's
  accoutrements;
I am not in the least afraid of these giant sharks which
I am not one of those sad fools who say to God
I am not one of those who can calmly watch as his children explode
I am not proud of the fact that I detest women and children.
I am not remotely interested in f——ing pandas.
I am not remotely interested in young people as such.
I am not very interested in sticking to the floor.
I am not widely regarded as a cuddly person, I concede;
I am not yet completely conscious of my own genius;
I am now convinced that my life's work is, broadly, a heap of
  rubbish;
I am of Noblivia.
I am of No Fixed Abode.
I am of Nolivia.
I am of Oblivia. Alternatively,
I am of Wobblivia. Look it up on the map.
I am only trying to work out what it is you want.

I am only writing to ask you, erm, for the fleeting use of your body
I am passionately interested in finding some academic sinecure
I am perhaps this century's leading Oblivian
I am quite astonishingly uninterested in tarts.
I am rather hoping this language will soon die out.
I am – Sir Henry Raeburn!
I am sitting behind a bar in a deep puddle
I am slowly groping forward
I am so powerful that I don't even need to exist.
I am sorry, Snorri, but it's not going to be me
I am speaking from an unknowable but nonetheless authentic space
I am still not quite completely bored by Art, Science and Love.
I am sublimely indifferent to money.
I am terrified of being arrested for the size of my private parts.
I am terrified of female sexuality.
I am the erection in the lifeboat.
I am the madman in the Pando District,
I am the source of an inexhaustible interest
I am the Way, the Truth and the Laugh
I am the Way, the Truth and the Loaf
I am the winning ticket which Oblivia did not even buy!
I am tied, O Lord, to your enormous pillar
I am tired of doing the right thing all the time.
I am trying my level best to get rid of some of my houses.
I am turning into a millionaire far, far too slowly
I am turning into an old person without having signed the right
    forms!
I am uninterested in all but the local botany.
I am well aware that I have a great deal going for me.
I apologise for setting your children on fire. It was
I assume you are in favour of worldwide famine?
I assure you I am not paranoid in the slightest. No.
I assure you, said Almighty God, I am not being ironic;
I awoke one morning to find myself almost entirely invisible.
I believe his last words were to praise the smell
I believe in Oblivia, because
I believe in the hereafter, although I do not know
I believe it greatly amused my mother at the time
I believe I've already said, Vince, how happy I was in that garden.
I bought all the recommended books. What a waste of time that was!

I can assure you (as my dying mother told me) I had no idea
I can do anything. But no-one seems to have noticed.
I can hardly believe that I am eighty-five years old
I cannot believe that the crude mechanics of sex
I cannot claim to be particularly enormous
I cannot quite believe in the beauty of the lirk
I cannot quite understand the fondness I feel for spiders.
I cannot think – no, I cannot think –
I can see I have been defeated by respectable society.
I can't believe how stupid I have been
I can't believe I really said that – did I? –
I can't believe that I am nearly forty years old;
I can't believe that women could have done all this for me –
I can't believe that women could have done all this to me –
I can't get these bloody openings out of my mind.
I can't quite work out whether the problem's at the top or the
    bottom.
"I can't see how *anyone* could be interested in schoolboys.
I claim little credit for having such an enormous tool.
I come from nothingness and I go back to it
I concede that I must be descended from some very unlikeable
    people.
I confess, Sir, it was I who defaced your pornographic magazine.
I consider myself to have been quite unforgivably betrayed.
I continually think of those who very possibly had syphilis.
I continue to see a difference between success and failure.
I could never be much in favour of shooting fogs.
I couldn't bear it if such were the case. It must therefore surely be
    otherwise –
I could sit laughing at animals for hours.
I could tell even from the way that she was lying
I could try to climb over it, I suppose,
I'd always assumed the Muse was supposed to stroll about in the buff;
I dare say, if the stars were a stream of coffee,
I dare say if you found someone making love to your new handbag
I dare say much less than a thousand women
I decided to simplify matters by trying to kill him or her.
I deny absolutely that I am in any way a woman
I deny that I really had a middle-class upbringing.
I did not ask to be given these seven or eight magnificent attributes.

I did not ask to be made a colossal genius, did I? No.
I did not realise that I was a truly great writer
I did not think that the bunk in which I was conceived
I didn't ask to be made sexually irresistible.
I didn't even realise I was doing it until
I disapprove of all forms of injustice whatsoever.
I discovered she had shaved her private parts in the National
    Library;
I discovered the happy phrase in a black book
I do not admire you any the less because of your cretinous inability
I do not admire you the less because of your insane political views
I do not ask to be loved by absolutely everyone.
I do not care if I never see your apparatus again.
I do not care in the least if certain filthy journalists
I do not deny that a certain proud Inca ferocity
I do not deny that several dozen Indian women
I do not expect to win prizes for my fairness of mind.
I do not expect to win prizes for my highly acute hearing.
I do not give a shit about the so-called Nobel Prize;
I do not give the universe permission to kill me.
I do not greatly like the Past's enormous, over-active penis.
I do not hugely favour the Future's enormous feet.
I do not like the smell that History in general gives off.
I do not like to say that Oblivia has failed me.
I do not like to see people erupting in spots – particularly
I do not mind being the father of some six or seven children;
I do not much object to being mistaken for a God.
I do not need to be told that even child rapists are human.
I do not see why ignorance and cowardice
I do not think of myself as belonging to a language group.
I don't even know if I should be doing this.
I don't feel all that clean
I don't know. Did Man fall or was he pushed?
I don't know how all these things got here, do I?
I don't know how those bloody buildings got here, do I?
I don't know what's going on. So what? I never have done.
I don't know where all my children have disappeared to;
I don't know who you are, but I will say this:
I don't know why the tiny breasts of not unintelligent women
I don't know why the Universe has to piss so much.

I don't mind admitting that your wallpaper excites me profoundly,
    Darling.
I don't much like membranes. Never have done. Never will.
I don't quite understand why, in my dream, your ceiling
I don't quite understand why, in my dream, your feet
I don't remember; no, I don't remember at all
I don't see how we can possibly expect to get away with this.
I don't see why my complete lack of interest in your career
I don't suppose I could be dead already, could I?
I don't think we can quite say the whole thing is a farce.
"I don't want to hear about it!" said God to his Creation.
I don't want to think of it! No! I don't want to think of it!
I do obey him for he has the cash
I doubt if I had even heard of China
I doubt if mankind is quite as clever as all that.
I doubt if you can tell, before you read the rest of the poem,
I dreamed I could hear your dead voice whispering to me;
I dreamt I was in Paris again; and this time
I drink to excess because I am essentially a democrat.
I encountered the essentially transcendent last Tuesday evening.
I fall to the floor. The terrible pain sighs and subsides.
I farted, and fell senseless to the ground,
I farted – and the Albatross fell dead into the sea.
If, as now seems to be the case, Jesús, the reports of your death
If Brazil were again to become a single vast lake,
If by some mischance, O Universe, you do not think you need me,
If by "understanding women", you mean
I fear I am now a little too old to die young;
I fear I lack the one essential quality
I fear I may be exposing myself too much
I fear I may have laughed once too often
I fear it was when I first had sex with my bank manager
I fear it was when I first had sex with my deputy bank manager
I fear the whole universe must be a swindle of some sort.
I feel a desperate urge to grill your new secretary
I feel a mighty affection for these small, useless creatures
I feel as if I have fallen down a tiny little hole
I feel a sudden, renewed urge not to commit suicide.
I feel incredibly randy this morning. But who cares?
I feel I should be doing less with my life than this.

I feel sad. My thoughts are in Tarabuco.
I feel sorry for more or less everyone.
I feel that the world pays me far too much money
I fell to the floor, screaming, for some reason or other.
If ever I lose interest in the sacred junction
If ever a man made a mess of his life, that Jesus character did.
If ever a man made a mess of his life, that Rimbaud did!
If forced to choose between my children and my new car,
If, for instance, the English had agreed to employ Columbus,
If God exists, He does so by sheer chance.
If God had hated us, then no doubt concentration camps
If God had not somehow wanted my child to die of bone-marrow
    cancer
If God had really hated the suffering of children
If God had really wanted you to be intelligent
If God had really wanted you to be intelligent, Father,
If God wanted to make the world he did not want
If I could have back all the time I spent thinking about you
If I could only come back to Earth after I had ceased to exist,
If I'd been Shakespeare's mistress, and my bust
If I had died last year – which, in fact, I nearly did –
If I had instead devoted all that time to admiring busts
If I had remotely realised how much work it would involve,
If I may be allowed to quote from the matchless language of
    Scripture:
If I may say so, Clarinda, thy bits are a bit inadequate.
If I must die in this prison, I will die very bravely.
If I must die, let me at least be no more dead than your guano,
I find ——'s poems particularly exciting, because
I find I am still thinking about that shepherd girl's mosquito bites.
I find it hard to believe that I am really twenty-four.
I find it hard to imagine *wanting* to be a snake.
I find —— ——'s poems particularly exciting, because
I find ——'s poems particularly exciting, because
I find the main problem with men is that they are forever
I find there is always another man already involved
I find the whole world just such a bloody embarrassment.
I find ——'s poems particularly unexciting, because
If I should die (not that I really expect to)
If I should sink through the ice and disappear,

If I should start to fart uncontrollably, think only this of me:
If it hadn't been these loonies, it would no doubt have been other
   loonies
If it isn't about having children, then what on earth is it about?
If I want to know what Shakespeare looks like, I glance in the
   mirror.
If I were not Oblivian – which is, of course, unthinkable –
If I were those three cherry blossoms and a dog-turd
If I wished to, I could scatter all your arguments like chaff.
If John Knox had rather a weakness for young Englishwomen,
If killing is wrong, then what does that make the Universe?
If, my captain, apopleptic on the peak of Popocatepetl,
If Oblivia were to be removed from this continent,
If one has to choose between DNA and God
If one's neighbour were to disappear completely overnight
If only I could care much less about
If only it could always be dawn, even when the sun is setting.
If only I were a little less intelligent
If only my first wife had had rather more money,
If only my fourth wife had not been *quite* such a money-grubber,
If only my second wife had had rather more money,
If only the Mother Superior had not been wearing that ape-mask
If only the Universe had been able to produce us properly!
If only we could *all* have had different fathers!
I forbid women to sully my grave by visiting it.
I for one shall never yield to f——ing threats of f——ing violence!
I found a condor's skull on the altiplano;
I found a flat in Hyndland, on an incomparably gentle hill
I found an abandoned aeroplane in my back garden;
I found someone else's wallet on the machair. (Great!)
If silence, exile, syphilis and cunning
If that noise just upstairs goes on for very much longer
If that old shitbag, Time, with his dusty, dodgy heart,
If the Good Lord finds starving children so rewarding,
If the morning sunlight is not shining into our kitchen
If the morning sunlight is not shining onto a fold
If the ochre slayer has problems keeping his trousers up
If there really were a crime of bestial stupidity,
If there were a Nobel Prize for genitalia,
If this is what a merciful God is like

If to the Muse I hand this large, unripe banana,
If trampled dung gives perfume, then the foot
If we do hate, it was taught us by our neighbours.
If we must murder each other, let us at least do so with love;
If we never argued, would we be worse or better?
If you are about to be born again now,
If you are about to be born now,
If you are awoken at midnight by the sigh of a passing horseman,
If you are woken at midnight by the fart of a passing horse,
If you could have waited till tomorrow, I wouldn't have been here.
If you don't mind, I'd rather not summon up things past just at the
    moment;
If you had not repeatedly hit me over the head with that fruit-bowl,
If you had the slightest inkling how often I piss in your sink,
If you really want to follow Jesus, my friend, then become a Jew.
If you too are a poet and suspect that your private parts
If you were the last woman on earth – which I'm sure you are not –
I get angry all the bloody time these days.
I get angry at the thought of how many poor people there are.
I get extremely angry at the thought of how many rich people
    there are.
Ignorant bastards! Why did you stop speaking Latin?
I greatly recommend the view from this slaughterhouse roof.
I had always hoped I would die before anything like this happened.
I had an auntie – Peggy – who worked in Duns for several years,
I had an uncle (Nicephorus) who worked in Dunn's for decades.
I had a vague intention of writing some really great stuff;
I had been rather hoping to be dead by now.
I had never played with a real angel's tail before.
I had three main reasons for going to Iona.
I had two main reasons for going to Zudañez.
I hated the plastic flowers in the corpse's hair;
I hate everyone at sight. It saves time and energy
I hate heat, and sunlight, and all that sort of nonsense;
I hate that ridiculous topaz-coloured poncho you bought
I hate the idea that cars lack even metal souls
I hate the way the local people run away from me here.
I hate women. No, wait a moment. I'll rephrase that.
I have absolutely no recollection whatsoever of the house where I
    was born.

I have absolutely nothing against the Jews personally.

I have absolutely nothing to say about myself.

I have a great weakness for a truly sensible crack

I have almost ceased to be terrified by the prospect of total extinction.

I have always been pretty much opposed to genocide;

I have always felt that Moses got it fundamentally wrong

I have always had rather a penchant for imaginary persons;

I have always thought that Othello was a total disgrace.

I have a peculiar fondness for certain ferns

I have been forced to conclude that my accountant is a psychopath.

I have been jailed more than once for no very good reason,

I have been seduced by the dappled sunlight;

I have been sexually active for the last eighty-five years.

I have been sexually active for the last five hundred years – [And, believe me, I wouldn't recommend it to anyone.]

I have been sexually active for the last five hundred years – [Or so it sometimes seems, when I look at my old diaries.]

I have been sexually active since the previous millennium.

I have been slightly ill for a ridiculously long while now;

I have been told that Joyce used an absolutely enormous pen

I have begun, on occasional mornings, to fall over again.

I have come here with great respect to piss on all that is dear to you;

I have come to the conclusion that, if I were God,

I have decided to be unbelievably brilliant today;

I have devoted far too much of my life

I have difficulty these days even remembering what my father looked like.

I have done much travelling among nearly exhausted mines;

I have done my best to go native on this barren shore.

I have emitted large amounts of gunk at one time or another;

I have felt vaguely ill for the last fifty-odd years;

I have fought the good fight and, in all obvious senses, lost.

I have good reason to suppose I must be dying;

I have gradually come to realise that everyone else is human.

I have grave doubts as to whether the so-called Bronze Age

I have grown tired of being a sort of lobster.

I have had a uniquely privileged insight into the Nature of God, Eva.

I have had enough of these dangerous, silver-tongued fools.

I have had minor sexual encounters in all the major South
    American countries,
I have had my life – or as much of it as I wanted –
I have hung up your photograph beside one of Jesus Christ's
    Mother;
I have learned more about human beings than I ever wanted to.
I have little desire to clean your anus further, O Universe!
I have lived a more or less posthumous existence.
I have long had the ambition to go to Mao's birthplace and spray
I have long since given up philosophy for the maracas;
I have long since nursed the ambition to go to Lenin's Tomb and,
    holding
I have made a list of my five hundred and ten favourite words:
I have met them, farting uncontrollably,
I have never attempted to deny that I idealise your third eye, have I?
I have never been much of a one for attending meetings;
I have never doubted that angels urinate in the suburbs;
I have never felt myself threatened by excessive adulation.
I have never for a moment claimed to be perfect; only
I have never for a moment denied that Shakespeare had talent.
I have never for a moment doubted that women exist.
I have never quite got the hang of public lavatories.
I have never seen a more obviously evil child
I have never spoken of women as dangerous drugs
I have nobly eluded the facile blandishments of fame.
I have no fear whatsoever of predatory sexual inverts.
I have no idea how many kinds of beaver are known to Science.
I have no idea how many kinds of heaven are known to Religion.
I have no special status in the universe. Have I?
I have not paid enough attention I know to this
I have not the least doubt that most of them would
I have no wish to hear more about your sexual frustrations.
I haven't a clue, actually,
I have observed you gazing silently at my pied parrot.
I have often felt that Death was wasted on the dying.
I have often thought that the colour of the loved one's eyes
I have often thought that the colour of the loved one's hair
I have often thought that the colour of the loved one's new
    underpants
I have often wished that excessive earthly beauty

I have only just this moment realised why women are so superior
    to men.
I have only once seen a naked sailor – and, quite frankly,
I have played with my life by now in most of the great temples
I have played with myself stoically in many foreign countries,
I have played with their lights by now in most of our finest
    buildings;
I have played with your perfect structures at various mundane
    addresses;
I have practically never beat my little son on the head; and yet,
I have rarely had much pleasure out of listening to old men fart.
I have reached that stage in life when one sits about, hoping for
    miracles;
I have retired from life – alas, without a pension.
I have risen far above the disgusting vulgarity
I have sometimes felt that Moses was lucky not to exist;
I have taken a leading part in many imperial processions;
I have to admit I am absolutely terrified
I have to admit I was absolutely terrified
I have to say I don't much like what the evening is doing.
I have toyed with the affections of the Cosmos as such
I have urinated against at least three of the world's great ruins;
I have waited in so many boring Art Galleries
I heard a low, godly rumble in the woods at sunset;
I heard a most interesting story recently about an extremely boring
    old sailor.
I heard a voice in my ear which cried out, "If
I heard some foreigners giggling in the Andes,
I hear priests pissing again and again in the sea of Time;
I hear the dead year climbing up my awkward staircase.
I hereby accuse you, Madam – if 'accuse' is quite the right word –
I hereby accuse you, Your Grace, of spitting into my soup.
I hereby declare, as a proud and committed monoglot,
I hereby tell the whole world that I am not heterosexual.
I hitched my destiny to the wrong butterfly entirely;
I hitched my destiny to the wrong flag entirely;
I hitched my destiny to the wrong flap entirely;
I hold no brief for the royal house of Spain. (Poofs!)
I hope I don't shit myself too spectacularly when I die.
I hope my carpet is not too bright for your forehead

I hope they don't let all the wrong sort of people into Heaven.
I incline to the view that the whole damn thing is absurd.
I insist that you treat my escapist fantasies as being beyond
    criticism!
I just happened to be hiding underneath the table
I just want to make people more or less impossibly happy.
I keep dreaming about you – don't pretend not to know that!
I keep getting these glimpses of a life I never had;
I keep hearing an imaginary telephone
I keep thinking it's Monday afternoon.
I keep thinking there is something I must have forgotten.
I knew I shouldn't have told Fate to kiss my arse
I knew it would be you. Yes. I just knew it would be you.
I know all about men.
I know all about women.
I know all about worms.
I know all about xylophones.
I know all there is to know about their emotional dishonesty,
I know all too well that there are those to whom my breath
I know all too well that there are those to whom my feat
I know all too well that there are those to whom my writings
I know I should be gathering up crumbs for the archaeologists
I know not why someone as complex as myself
I know of nothing more truly fascinating
I lay on my bed and fiddled nonchalantly
I lay there wide awake for a full week;
I leave it to others, Isaac, to finish the little I have left undone;
I leave it to others to count the numbers of pillars in our great
    churches.
I like some women so much that I forget
I like to suspend my wife out of the window whenever possible.
I like to try to be kind to other people.
I live in a world of my own. Yes. Why not join me?
Illimani looks in from the distance as you dry your hair
I'll keep the gold and silver. You can have the apes.
I'll never forget how my fifth wife so greatly enjoyed
I'll never forgive those morons for not making me anti-Pope *at least*.
I'll probably do it later.
I'll tell you what the difference is between men and women.
I long to go back to the Holy Land and f—— like a donkey

I looked again into my mirror and thought: Jesus!
I loved that topaz-coloured whatever-it-was of yours;
I loved you, you stupid tart: what more can I say?
I love having a warm part of the Universe to cling onto;
I love the incomparable names of Eolivia.
I love to explore cities furtively, disguised as a coffee dealer.
I love to explore the town furtively, disguised as Ernest
    Hemingway in drag;
I love trying to carry extremely tall women
I'm a bit worried about my exact ontological status.
I'm afraid I didn't even have time to start this poem.
I'm afraid I had expected a bit more than this.
I'm afraid I may be seriously under the influence of dregs.
I'm afraid I'm going to try to kill myself.
I'm afraid I must ask you, Deirdre, to send back all my bones
I'm afraid I seem to be going slightly berserk.
I'm afraid it's a rare woman who really deserves a pulpit.
I'm afraid I've just had another rather brilliant idea.
I'm afraid the goods are simply too expensive.
I'm almost certain this was the street she lived in.
I'm an old git! Even me! How did that happen?
I may have left a jar behind in Chuquisaca Province;
I'm dead. But you don't really want to hear about me, do you?
I'm desperate. Doesn't that mean anything to you?
I'm dying! Please help me! No?
I mean, these difficulties we have even in our dreams!
I mean to say, we've been wrong about *everything else.*
I met you so frequently then, when you were working in embassies,
I'm much like anybody else, even though
I'm not afraid of these ancient puffs. Why should I be?
I'm pleased to say I found your grandmother
I'm pleased to say I found your great-grandmother
Impossible? Of course it's impossible. What isn't?
I'm putting my back out for Jesus.
I'm sorry, sweetheart, but the sad fact is
I'm sure I can remember when this mountain used to be bigger.
"I'm sure there's something I've forgotten," thought God to
    himself.
I'm sure this carpet would look much nicer in the front room.
I'm sure this country was conquered by my father-in-law.

I must admit I was, to say the least, surprised
I must arise and go now, and repair to the Glasgow Sheriff Court;
I must ask you not to call me a "fat, perverted cretin".
I must beg you, Madam, not to throw your elf at me.
I must beg you never again to wipe your bum with my letters.
I must look absolutely fantastic in this uniform!
I must needs go out now and kill various tedious foreigners.
I must say I find it broadly encouraging
I must say, I think boredom is seriously under-rated.
I must say, on the whole, I rather approve of death.
I must say, the idea of inspecting Virginia Woolf's private parts
I'm very happy that I'm no longer sensationally attractive;
I'm very sorry: I thought you said "the Ancient Geeks".
In a fair fight, Truth will usually lose.
In all but three of the countries of South America,
In all my life, little or nothing so wonderful
In all these sunlit rooms where windows are shrieking
In another sense, I just haven't bothered to write them;
In a sense, this world is God's condom, isn't it?
In a sense, we are all exiled Oblivians.
In Athens, I locked myself in a public lavatory.
In Auschwitz, the old Jewish saying that 'God loves laughter'
In a world chock-full of threats, I stand up and proudly proclaim
Incomparable plenitude!
In deference to several more or less equally insane faiths,
Independence? No, no, no, no! Please – no! Anything but that!
I need a heron – an uncommon want, I concede;
Ineffable effulgence!
I never quite met the persons whom I thought I met;
I never saw either the father of my father
In every city in the world, all the bloody time,
In fact, as early as the eleventh century,
In fact, no-one has ever really been skilled in magic;
Ingavi! Name famous wherever on earth Liberty
In good old Boston, where a few dozen unrepresentative
    paedophile priests
In God I trust because Reality has failed me so badly.
In his troubling fresco, *St Columba Having a Quiet Tug*
I nipped downstairs for some bread and milk – but, unfortunately,
In Jerusalem, I locked myself in a public lavatory.

In Lourdes, I almost locked myself in a public lavatory.

In many ways, I am the troubled daughter I never had;

In most cases, of course, nothing gets written down;

In my dreams, you swell again to thrice your present size,

In my dreams, you were wearing much more expensive tights

I no longer see that couple who used to live across the street.

In our basic twenty-roomed house, set in barely a hundred acres,

I now cling to the faith doggedly, he said – without joy –

I now very much regret throwing your clothes out of that window.

In religion too it is very easy just to make things up.

In retirement, one after another thinks: "Did I really do that?"

In Rome, I locked myself in a public library.

Inside-out? Upside-down? What's the difference?

Inspecting my penis with growing horror in a friend's house,

In that glowing, golden kitchen above a lane

In that grim Russian tragedy, *A Month in the Same Pair of Underpants*,

In that parallel world of ours, where there are no bathrooms,

In the bookshop's challenging new *Mind, Body & Crap* section,

In the brilliance of the night, the Lord showed me a mystic ring.

In the end, everything is what it is, even ——.

In the end, everything will (oh, thank God!) be forgotten;

In the end of everything is the beginning of everything, Ben.

In the end, this has not very much to do with Bolivia.

In the end, we cannot do enough for Oblivia.

In the few surviving fragments of Eliot's *Kipping in the Cathedral*,

In the middle of the cemetery, a truly enormous obelisk

In the middle of the snow-drenched woods, I fell off my horse.

In the mirror, he watched the young doctor licking

In the morning light, a proud pair of Bolivians

In the morning, light came at a completely unknown angle

In the morning, lying out on the balcony again,

In the morning, sitting out on the balcony,

In the morning, yet again crawling out onto the balcony,

In the profounder sense, my country has never lost a war.

In the Sixteenth Century, when the British fleet

In the small kitchen, we laughed at *Gone With the Wind*

In the Vatican City, I locked myself into a public lavatory.

In the years when I used to be used as a sullen sexual plaything,

In this small kitchen, I have had unforgettable experiences.

In Thörshavn, I locked myself into a public library.

In Thunder Bay, I locked myself in a church;
In thy small bay, where men's hopes rest at anchor,
In Tipperary, I locked myself into the British Council offices.
Into the woods the furtive idolators dispersed;
In Tuxtla Gutiérrez, I locked myself into one of the Mayan ruins;
In *Under the Cardinal* by, I think, Christina Hole
In Verkhoyansk I locked myself out of my house. Bad move!
In Vijayanagar, I locked myself up in a Cultural Heritage office.
In which sacred book, my child, does a talking llama
In Würzburg, I locked myself out of a large, blue-painted house
In your broad streets, O Oblivia, one hundred thousand years ago,
In your grim country, (oh buffoons!) – the most ridiculously
    shaped in the whole world –
In Zagazig, I locked myself up in a tomb;
In Zürich, I inadvertently locked myself into a bank vault.
In Zürich, I was kept prisoner in a charming rococo church
I object to rich people, on principled, moral grounds.
I often think, Father, that those whose private parts have never
    been kissed
Iona is scarcely *quite* the place for a nudist beach.
I once had a summer job on an island I cannot now find.
I ought not to have undressed your daughter with these garden
    shears, I know;
I prefer my wife's v—— to the Taj Mahal;
I proclaim magnificent news to the whole world!
I proclaim to the whole world that I am completely heterosexual.
I promise you poetry, Vince, until you are tired of it!
I proudly say to Pride: God bids thee go!
I pulled away some old railings, and climbed the modest wall
I quite like the rag-tag uniform of the universe.
I raise my fist to the United States and say, "F——
I ran as fast as I could down the bright, moonlit stairway,
I ran up the secret ladder, intent on a chaste form of splash
I rather fear I might drop dead on your new carpet;
I rather like the idea that cars have liquid souls.
I rather presume my parents at least *liked* each other.
I rather resent having been constructed by genitalia.
I rather resent having been constructed with genitalia.
I really didn't think I would ever be doing this.
I really didn't think we would ever be doing this.

I reckon we still have to be a good few hundred short
I recognise this moon from high Oblivia.
I recommend the view from this church roof.
I refuse to acknowledge Time. No. Kindly piss off!
I refuse to allow myself to be annihilated twice.
I refuse to see myself as a physical being.
I refuse to worry about my pretty little head about mere reality.
I rejoice to High Heaven that all my children are gay!
I remember absolutely nothing whatsoever about it.
I remember how often in Garnethill I used to run from my Auntie
I remember how once, quite accidentally, a large
I remember how once, when I visited a French restaurant in
    Germany,
I remember how once, when I visited a German restaurant, in
    Greece,
I remember how once, when I visited a Greek restaurant in France,
I remember how surprised I was to discover I had pubic hair.
I remember how, the first time I visited a Thai restaurant,
I remember how, the last time I visited Greece,
I remember how, the second time I visited Thailand,
I remember how we found each other in a dimly lit basement.
I remember how you once burst into the room, screaming
I remember making a clear decision not to do this.
I remember once how a five litre container of urine
I remember – or do I, in fact? No; on second thoughts, I don't.
I remember that time I opened the door and discovered
I said: I'll do it later. I remember that.
Is Allan the most boring character Mankind has ever invented?
I sat down in the garden and realised I loved nearly everything.
I saw her again some twenty years later. Jesus!
I saw the blood pour down his much respected shirt-front
I saw the Lord standing precariously on the toilet-bowl;
I say this quite forthrightly to the Kremlin:
I say this quite forthrightly to the Vatican:
I say this quite forthrightly to the White House:
I say this quite forthrightly to whoever runs the Yoker Literature
    Festival:
I see all of space and time in the world of a single cough;
I seem to have lost all the power in my feet.
I see my Oblivia now, a surprising puzzle

I see someone else has just been found hanged in Balmoral.
I sense a power vacuum
I shall arise and go now to the Lago de Baja Huinaimarca,
I shall die triumphant in the hop of immortality;
I shall die triumphant in the shop of immorality;
I shall never be exhausted, so long as my Bolivia
I shall not waste one second more of my life
I shall perhaps find out after I cease to exist
I shall probably go down to Potosì tomorrow.
I shall tear down this old wall with my remaining hand, if need be,
I shook you noisily while the TV nearby was showing a silent film.
I should have talked to that strange guest who visited me last night.
"I should never have stayed on in this bloody country!"
I simply cannot get my eyes to open again.
I simply refuse to believe that bacteria
I shall never again be surprised by anything my children do.
Is it an old fence? The age of the fence doesn't matter.
Is it me? Or is Glencoe not in fact profoundly
Is it my fault if bringing up children is women's work?
Is it possible that I am not really here?
Is it wrong to like hearing of the deaths of a dear friend?
Is Life not a joke which one can eternally repeat?
Is life a mystery to the insects? How could it be?
I snap my wiry Oblivian fingers at the tiny volcanoes
Isn't there a bookshop *anywhere* in this bloody city?
I sold my soul in Stirling, the oldest city in Europe;
I sometimes feel I should apologise for the future.
I sometimes feel limitless. Therefore I must, in some sense,
I sometimes suspect there are palaces hidden on all these
    mountains;
I sometimes think I should never have loved any of them;
I sort of think I've done it, but that no-one else has noticed.
I sort of vaguely expected to be massively famous;
[Is that one line or two, Ken?]
Is there a more gifted thinker than myself alive at present?
Is there anyone else in the house? No? Good. Then let's begin.
Is there no before and after even within the dream?
Is there some good reason why I can't find my favourite shirt?
Is there some place around here called Graig Roan?
Is this really the same moon that shines in Antarctica?

I still exist. It is often rather a disappointment
I still like to dress up as a monk as often as I can.
I still like to dress as a monkey as often as I can.
I still like to dress up as an ex-king whenever I can.
I stood beside the bed, shaking uncontrollably.
I stood beside your bed last night; but, no doubt fortunately,
I stood on the bridge of the future, screaming "Ponces!"
I stopped my car in the evening, high among the clouds.
I suddenly heard her shrieking in the next room,
I suddenly heard him laughing in the next room,
I suddenly remembered what it had really been like.
I suddenly remembered who the moon's face reminded me of.
I suppose you must think you're really very smart, don't you?
I suspect Eternity itself wouldn't be long enough
I suspect I am just about to explode into action.
I suspect I am still not dead yet.
I suspect I have almost unbearably attractive ankles.
I suspect I have rather a lot in common with Almighty God.
I suspect I very nearly did something quite remarkable
I suspect I very possibly idealise fireworks.
I suspect there are probably fewer things on heaven and earth
I take back what I said about your knees.
I take it you are in favour of world poverty, are you?
It all began with a rush of blood to the head.
It all dances around in different shapes
It always takes time to work out what the original belief must have
    been.
Italy? Huh. What did Italy ever do?
It depends what you mean by "success", I suppose.
It happened in Puerto Izozog.
It happened somewhere else.
It happened suddenly.
It happened very suddenly.
It happened. What else need I say?
It happens that sometimes I tire of being half an idiot.
It has very often occurred to me that sex
I think children are rubbish, basically. Don't you?
I think I can recognise the Impossible when I see it, dear.
I think I'd prefer it if it were in the plural.
I think I'd prefer it if I were in the plural.

I think I may claim to have read all the really important books
    twice.
I think I may have developed here a quite magnificent tool
I think I may predict, with no little confidence,
I think I must be off my f——ing head
I think I prefer you in those knickers after all.
I think I should tell you that my father, though a wonderful person,
"I think I should warn you that my husband is, essentially, a fascist,"
I think men are rubbish.
I think of you, I may say, almost as a good friend.
I thought I could walk on water till a woman pulled my plug;
I thought I had already produced my masterpiece
I thought I heard a voice crying in my ears: "Write! Write!"
I thought I wanted to spend my whole life more or less underneath
    his
I thought I was Oblivian. But it turns out I am Japanese!
I thought I could earn a living just by being me;
I thought there was a plastic flower in the corpse's anus
I thought you loved me.
I thought you loved me. In fact, I thought the *world* loved me.
It is absolutely false to call this country "cold"!
It is all a poor translation from mathematics.
It is all simply too complicated for me.
It is almost as if Jesus had the Oblivians in mind
It is always an overstatement to say that the Universe has come to
    an end
It is always morning in the Albivian poem.
It is an exaggeration to say I dislike everybody.
It is as well to remember that the condor is a type of vulture.
It is certainly not true that my father was the town drunk.
It is claimed that some women, when wearing the crinoline,
It is cold. It is, in fact, extremely cold.
It is difficult to believe that all the Caesars shat.
It is easier to be cynical than to understand the subject –
It is enough for me to be an incredibly great writer;
It is hard to respect a shit-smeared, grinning drunk.
It is important to propitiate the non-Existent, because
It is impossible *not* to influence the course of the world.
It is impossible to believe that all the Chinese Emperors farted.
It is just one bloody twinge after another.

It is just one more bloody twange after another.
It is less life I am tired of, than
It is my profound and sincere belief that things are not what they are.
It is not easy to believe that all these saints and mystics felt
It is not exactly that I wish we had never met.
It is not for me to descant on my finer qualities;
It is not for me to say how much value there may be in what I write.
It is not for me to say you are round the bend;
It is not I but the world which is the pervert.
It is not obligatory to understand one's own life, is it?
It is not so much that my homeland owes me a living
It is not that I love you less — though, in fact, I do —
It is now the duty of the authentic Bolivian genius
It is now time for me, I guess, to deliver my higher message.
It isn't an Ancient Mariner
It is only right that I now suffer for all the drink and debauchery
It is part of my proud, ancient culture to use such direct words
It is perhaps an old man's privilege to stick flowers
It is said, he did not smile for fifty-one years.
It is simple. You are taking a fiction far too seriously.
It is simply a fact that most other men are absolute bastards.
It is sometimes a bad mistake to adopt a snake.
It is the astonishing variety of human experience
It is true. He was a very happy pervert.
It is 'true' only in a rather specialised sense of the term.
It is very many years now, darling, since last I had a serious sexually
    transmitted disease.
It is vitally important to have contempt for the right things.
It is well attested that smoke can billow out of God's nostrils,
It is your own choice which forces God to make you do what you
    must;
It may be thought that in some measure I have succeeded
It may or may not have been William the Silent who said
It must have been burning all night — yet I knew nothing about it! —
It must have dropped to the floor from my sleeping hand!
It never crossed my mind that I might forget
I told them the truth and they cried out: "Shut up, Poof!"
I too am an intellectual giant on the grand scale.
I too am now in the grip of certain overwhelming urges.
I too, like Wilde, have done a terrible thing.

It pains me greatly, to think of how very young prostitutes
It pains me much, dear friend, to have to say that your poetry
It proved to be impossible to switch the machine off.
It's all your fault for believing what I said to you.
It's always a little upsetting when you put your clothes back on.
It's as much a question of interplay as anything else.
It seemed that out of *Bu Pa* I escaped
It seems I have done no good for forty-odd years.
It seems only reasonable that these immortal thoughts of mine
It seems that the Ancient Israelites were never in Egypt as such.
It seems there are some who suppose that their underpants are
    haunted;
It seems to me that we are a sort of cuddly toy
It seems we have to leave before we have quite found the entrance.
It seems you and I must come from the same slum.
It should not be thought, simply because I am called Jesus,
"It's like a lottery – except there are really no prizes –
It's not illegal to make less noise, you know.
It's not that I'm insensitive. It's just that I couldn't care less
It's silly – but, alas, I do it all the time.
It's simple. The woman is mad.
It's terribly nice of you to bother, but
It's the single extra fart that causes the damage.
It turns out he was a caveman after all!
It was a July morning, as I saw rise above the roof
It was all for a piece of fruit
It was always my hope to be overwhelmingly attractive
It was always such a delight to
It was at just that time that the Saviour of No-one
It was easier to be Ishmael. After all, he didn't exist.
It was, I believe, the Creator of the Universe who once remarked
It was, I think, from Stalin that I learned my immense compassion.
It was, I think, those seven very great British and Irish poets,
It was neither the words, nor the tune, nor the waving of the panties
It was never my wish to be overwhelmingly attractive
It was not death, for I fell out
"It was nothing," she said – gently releasing her grip
It was not I who stole
It was not me who stole
It was only then that he noticed his horse had feet;

It was while climbing Ben Nevis (famously, England's highest
    mountain)
It was while singing the *Marks & Spencer's Knickers Come-All-Ye*
It was worth writing the whole thing just for that one line.
It will surely never occur to most people
It would be rash, I suppose, to call the Universe a failure.
It would have crushed me if she too had said: "Don't do that!"
It would surely be much more fitting for God to believe in Bach.
I understand nothing. But then, who does?
I urinate each day; therefore I am essentially a non-physical being.
I used to think that everything ends too quickly.
I used to wear the same vest for months in a row.
I usually welcome in the New Year by paying a woman to shave
I've always had a sneaking ambition to be murdered by small-
    breasted Indians.
I've done it! I've had them both! (Unless, perhaps,
I've found that women are always already involved with somebody
    else;
I've grown accustomed to her garden gate in the orchard
I've had another idea! I've had another idea!
I've had everything I hoped for. (What a disaster!)
I very much fear that Almighty God is now trapped in Hell,
I very much like observing your nostrils while you sleep;
I very much like recording her expressions while she sleeps;
I very much like to watch you doing that.
I visited you astrally last Tuesday. Did you notice?
I waited for you in that room some fifty-three years or so.
I want it to be the case! What further "proof" does one need?
I want to be carried to your bed, dropped there, and climbed on
    top of,
I was alone a couple of evenings ago at the *Teatro Obliviano*,
I was found in a cardboard box at the age of thirty-four.
I was having a tough shit, when I heard a disembodied voice
I was in Peru for the best part of a full day
I was kept chained in a cupboard for over two full years,
I was not surprised to see so many mirrors walk down the street
I was relaxing in a thermal shower with a few delightful young
    friends,
I was shocked by the deterioration visible in his features
I was so naive! How did I survive at all?

I was suddenly seized by the ineffable majesty of God's hand (if
   that's what it was),
I was wrong (I see that now) to stand up and shout: "Stop! Liar!
   Turd!"
I watched your face for hours. I could have done that
I wear this present of hers inside-out because
I well remember my grandparents telling me to shut up
I well remember telling my grandparents to shut up
I well remember that morning when I drank fifty-three whiskies
I went in a sort of dream to the house of the Konitzers,
I went into my hotel-room at, say, almost eleven o'clock;
I went out into the garden and thought: I have lost everything!
I went right up to the so-called "Great Author" and said to him,
   with complete honesty:
I, who know what it is to fail to climb the great mountains,
I will not waste one second more of my miserable life
I wish at least half of these young people would go away and die.
I wish I had met you exactly nine years earlier;
I wish my former lovers were all dead too;
I wish the whole world were as convincing as my new socks.
I wish to say the magical word which will start
I wish to snap the knicker-elastic of Fate.
I wish to snap the knicker-elastic of God.
I wish to snap the knicker-elastic of that strange little secretary
I wish you would stop giving me such healthy food to eat!
I wish you would stop saying "No, it isn't!" all the time.
I woke up again – and found myself still completely unknown.
I wonder if Darius ever had diarrhoea.
I wonder if I might be allowed, Madam, to make a perhaps
   startling suggestion.
I wonder sometimes if Jesus might not really have been a woman.
I wonder what her name was.
I worshipped the ground on which you sat and screamed
I would advise all the tributaries of the Amazon
I would call the universe only minimally acceptable, Norbert.
I would do anything for you, O My Country – except perhaps
I would like nothing whatsoever to be known about me.
I would like to eventurate your grogeous nubariatum! Yeagh!
I would much prefer it if you did not call them, goolies.
I would neither have laughed nor wept nor

I would never be able to forgive myself if I beat an old woman (or
   indeed, man) to death.
I would not quite call Chesterton a porn merchant;
I would not quite say I had had no life at all.
I wouldn't say I was exactly *looking forward* to death.
I would quite like to die in any palace in Munich.
I would rather not say
I would rather not say what my idea of perfect happiness is.
I xenogenate here – but who cares what I do?
I yodel because – but who cares why I do it?
I zeteticate here – if there ever was such a word.
Izzumfantarticasiphendolandro? Yes… Well… Frankly, I doubt it,
   my dear.

Jack the Ripper? Whenever I hear the name,
Jalap, the purgative root of an Ipomoea or *Exogonium*,
'Japanese women in little kilts'? Whenever I hear the phrase,
Japan! Were it not that your females so enthusiastically
J.C. was a two-legged animal who, of course, eventually died.
Jenny farted uncontrollably when we met,
Jesus Christ? Huh. I kent his faither.
Jesus Christ was, like most people, politically more or less clueless.
Jesus does not have a realistic personality.
Jesus doesn't seem to have had very many friends.
Jesus slipped off into a deeper part of the bushes
"Jesus" was, it seems, a very common Jewish name;
Jesus was no more a Christian than Pontius Pilate was.
John Nox? John Nix? John Nux?
Jones, my next-door neighbour, old Fred, who was so quiet,
Joy, Joy in La Paz now!
Julia, there is something I simply *have* to tell you.
Just after the Manchu people had conquered the whole of China,
Just a note, dear friend, to say that I have not had your wife
Just as worn-out clothes can suddenly become new,
Just for a turd in a top-hat he left us;
Just one more lunatic, one that looked round, baffled,

Keenly aware as I am of the deep spiritual inadequacies of other
    people,
Keeping silent, I would be failing in my duty
Kept chained out in the tropical rains for weeks,
Kierkegaard's third eye, if his doctor is to be believed,
Kill me instead, if you must have a victim. Yes.
Kindly accept my apologies, dear Cunninghame Graham,
Kindly bring over here to me at least half a litre of *chicha*!
Kindly do not fling any more of that shit at me!
Kindly do not talk to me about England again quite yet.
Kindly feel quite free to piss off at any point
Kindly shut up, Mr President, with your pointless and rhetorical
    questions,
King Arthur a Bolivian? Although, perhaps, at first sight
King David couldn't hold a tune to save his life.
King David is hardly a historical character.
Known only to God – (that is to say, unknown) –
Kublai Khan intended, once he had conquered Japan,

Lake Titicaca is wonderfully calm tonight, isn't it?
Lana, if only the whole world were as delightful
Land of strong drink, strange talk, and child molesters!
Lane. Perhaps. Sunlight. Morning. Kitchen. ——.
La Paz! Twin City of Mecca, Lanark, and Jerusalem!
La Paz! Your very name is made for women's voices.
Largs itself, I should say, has little to show more fair
Last night, on the Avenida Oblivia, a man stopped me and asked:
Last night, the woman I love said: "Listen, Shortarse.
Last Sunday, as I passed water behind the new Jesuit church,
Last Sunday morning, as I worshipped at the old Jesuit church,
Last week, I bought a pair of really nice new shoes.
Lately a cabbalistic book was written entitled *Bo / Ob*.
Later that same evening, when all his companions were drunk,
Later that same morning, when his disciples were still drunk,
Leaking various fluids, we seep to the life invisible;
Leave it with me. I'll see what I can do.
Leave! Whatever you might have in your pockets
Lenin, from the tasty brains of dead, unimportant people

Leonardo? Michelangelo? Huh. Apart from anything else,
Let all astrologers, barbarians and idiots keep away
Let me be quite specific about what I intend to do with you.
Let me, I beg you, O Muse, begin this epic about poetry,
Let me just get this straight. When you called me "repulsive"
Let me just take a wild guess here.
Let me risk opening this right out to its fullest extent
Let me share with you my opinion of various French cheeses.
Let me tell you (yet again) why *nothing* does not exist.
Let nobody leave this country on any pretext whatsoever!
Let no-one ever claim I demanded worship.
Let our seventeen-languaged country, which the whole world
Let's drive over the pavement here. Nobody important will mind;
Let's kick Space in the balls, me boys,
Let them call me a "shit in the grand tradition" if they wish!
Let them say what they like about Honorificabilitudinis Avenue.
Let them say what they like about Urtilanchtetlanochtli Boulevard.
Let them say what they like about Wilton Street.
Let there be no mistake about what I mean:
Let us be perfectly clear about one thing at least:
Let us glorify the non-existent forever.
Let us hymn that gap through which He
Let us make no more jokes about women in unlit hotel basements.
Let us not descend yet again to mere verbal abuse.
Let us not treat truth as we treated the Indians.
Let us now praise not particularly famous bores.
Let us pray fervently to God that what happened didn't happen.
Let us talk nonsense on several quite different planes at once,
Life. A charming little strip down a back lane somewhere.
Life does not come much better than this, I thought to myself
Life has rarely sunk in properly even by the time we die;
Life is a sort of perpetual embarrassment
Life is a wonderful board-game – but where are the rules?
Life is a wonderful board-game which has not yet quite been
    perfected;
Life is completely unlike a transient vapour
Life is more like the notes for a biography
Life is unreal, is it? Compared to what?
Life may be cheap – but these life-jackets are grossly over-priced.
Life without women anywhere is hardly life at all, is it?

Like a doctor, dear, who each day must inspect
Like Burns, I too have suffered a very bad knee injury.
Like God, I by no means abhor the virgin's womb.
Like Jesus, I have no very clear source of income.
Like many, I suspect that Heaven will be rather dreadful.
Like many people who have lost an arm (or a leg)
Like most men, I secretly desire to urinate out of windows;
Like most who have collected thousands of birds' eggs
Like Mozart, Newton, Dewar or Leonardo, I have now reached
    the stage
Like so many religious people, I had lost the will to live
Like that young child who said to the Emperor: "Pervert!"
Like to the gentle dove who shits from its branch all morning
Like you, Madam, I am quite incapable of lying.
Listen. Every single word of every sacred text
Listen. I have been a World Cup semi-finalist – (twice!) –
Listen. It's not too difficult. What is not known is not known.
Listen, pervert. I am a tall, proud, male, Bolivian indigene.
Listen. That was a perfectly good pair of trousers.
Listen. Why not stuff your vision of suffering humanity
Literature? Yes, yes, yes, yes. So what?
Little did I think (when I wrote my Snogs of Oblivia)
Little internal flickers, like tiny flashes of memory,
Little piranha fish, what basically kind and loving intelligence made
    thee?
Loch Lomond (which is, by some way, the largest lake in England)
Lo! God wearing a nappy, and needing it changed at once!
Long may thy glorious banners proudly wave, O Woblivia!
Look, Adolf – couldn't we just go off somewhere a bit quieter,
Look, chum. If this is who I think it is,
Look. If I absolutely must suffer for my loyalty,
Look, if one lot didn't like them, the other lot wouldn't grow
    them at all.
Look. I know I like your trade-mark too much.
"Look. I'm married. I can't do that any more,"
Look: I'm very sorry to be tedious about all this,
Looking fitter than ever after his last heart attack,
Looking for fleas, I instead discovered a lizard. Wow!
Look – it might not matter much to you
Look, Lord – I am doing good! Can I have my reward now please?

Look! Morning! Snow! And you still have a glory hole, don't you?
Look. People do not want to have their noses rubbed in the truth.
Look! The rain falls on you too. Such lethal ignorance!
Look there! As if one perfect detail weren't enough,
Look. Whether Shakespeare died of syphilis or drink
Lopez! Unbending and devoted son of the Church!
Lord Byron suggests somewhere that Mohammed was a cuckold.
Lord, could you not have placed me in some other, safer garden?
Lord, even though your indwelling power sustains all my acts,
Lord God, thy all-sustaining tool
Lord, help me try to understand why I fart so much.
"Lord, I am your creature. What so should I do next?" asked
    Lucifer.
Lord! Perhaps you wonder why we draw to your attention to
    things [Which must in fact be exactly what You have arranged?]
Lord! Perhaps you wonder why we draw to your attention to
    things [Which you must know already? But you must know that
    already too.]
"Lord?" said Abraham. "Did I hear you quite right there?"
"Lord," said Adam. "This creature here has just called me a poof."
Lost among the wreckage of a dazzling civilisation,
Lo, the harsh maniac, with enormous feet,
Loudly and proudly farting down by the *yunga*,
Lucifer! I suppose you must think you are very, very smart.
Lyell and Hutton, those two great Irish geologists,
Lying on the floor, completely covered by chicken-shit,
Lying underground for century after century,

Madam, if I may say so, there is a Venus fly-trap
Madam, if I may say so, there is something very crude
Madam, if I scribbled my name upon your mother's buttocks,
Madam, if I seemingly half-transgressed the Laws of Decorum,
Madam, if the sound of my humble cracked mouth organ
Madam, I have sometimes thought it might be very nice
Madam, the esteemed (or should I perhaps say "the steamed"?)
Madam, this is far from being the worst thing that has happened to
    me.
Madam, thoughts of music, cream, your hips, grass and Paradise

Madam, when at your wedding party I heard myself say, "Let's do it now!"
Madam, when I remember how your Ming snuff boxes
Madam, when I remember how your wings
Madam, when I suspended you by your heels over that balcony,
Madam, while you and I were banging away so agreeably
Make me, oh Lord, your five and a half amp fuse,
Make no mistake. I have declared War to the Death on (Late) Capitalism.
Manly-muscled, masculine, male-marvellous, mild my Mark (O! mark! me!)
Man's life is a sort of fart in a dream;
Many have commented on how Lenzie and La Paz
Many have commented on how Peking and La Paz
Many of the African slave-traders who converted to Islam
Maria, get out of the garden while you still can.
Matchless city! Well indeed wert thou named after Peace!
Matey, the chap thou art addressing don't exist no more.
Maybe I talk too much? No. No. Surely not.
Maybe it *was* all rubbish after all?
Maybe I've just been meeting the wrong sort of women entirely;
Maybe the Lord God has just been imagining things.
Meeting you again on the day after we had virtually had sex, I assumed
Men are from the earth. As, indeed, are women.
Men of Oblivia! Women of Oblivia! Children of Oblivia!
Men? Men?
Mere children decide whether my works will be published or not.
Merely because a country has had a few hundred insurrections,
Merely because a great mind kills a few million people,
Merely because I have written four or five novels about adolescent youths,
Merely because I insist on being paid in dollars
Merely because I once worshipped a certain child,
Merely because of a few perhaps unguarded remarks about Jews and Africans,
Merely because she once caught me urinating into her favourite pot-plant
Merely because the machine may have exploded in mid-air,
Midnight. How many a dull and sickly member

Midnight. How many others are weeping even now in this suburb?
Might everything not in fact be something else?
Might I be allowed to tell you what to do with your Canal?
Millions have been killed by now for mistranslations.
Milton! Personally I am quite glad you're dead.
Modigliani, James Moffat, Mohammed, Molière, Molotov,
    Moltke,
Mohammed, like all the rest of us, was a two-legged mammal who
    died
Mohammed, who many have claimed was completely illiterate,
Mohammed, who some have claimed cannot possibly have been
    illiterate,
Mohammed, who some have claimed might have been both
    literate and illiterate,
Mohammed, who some have claimed was extremely tall and
    noble-looking,
Montevideo! Although a highly gifted pederast once
More than anything else, I would now like to go slightly deaf.
More than forty-nine years ago, you heard it
Moses, reluctant to look directly at the woman's backside,
Most marriages, I suspect, never actually happen.
Most of the clouds I have seen seem to travel in crowds;
Most of the great romantic gestures end up as a matter of some regret.
Most of the Koran is as factual as the genies
Most of the people who are fallen in love with don't quite exist.
Most of the women I have ever loved have now had children;
Most people are not who most other people take them for.
Most Saints know little or nothing about the real world.
Most Scriptures demonstrate an appalling shortage of mushrooms;
Most unexpectedly, the sacred damsel burst into tears.
Most women are, alas, as tedious as most men.
Mother – help me! What has happened to my private parts?
Mother, when you collapsed dead on the floor,
Moths, I find, are so entrancingly easy to kill!
Mozart! Mozart!
Mozart? Never heard of him,
Mr Hutton enjoyed, it is said, the company of intelligent women.
Much as an absent-minded priest in a brothel
Much as an archangel with overweight buttocks
Much as one never phuts the woman one loves, unless

Much have I travelled in the tin-producing areas,
Much of his work was in fact written by somebody else.
Much seems to happen that God does not want to happen.
"Mummy, why is that woman kissing that man's feet?"
Murdering people in an essentially loving, tolerant way
Mustapha, who often slept rough with his warrior companions,
Must you keep plucking your nipples from my boneless gums?
My advice to you is this: it is better to stay unknown,
My brain is plastic. So then; tell me from where
My daughter is quite worried about her pubic hair.
My daughter's friend was strangely surprised by her pubic hair.
My dear friend, for many years now we have shared visions
   through the post;
My dear Homeland! Mother of Art, Science, Law, Culture and Rest!
My dear Homeland! Saviour of World Civilisation!
My dear Homeland! The entire world watches you and thinks
My entire life has been a bad career decision.
My father and your father are in Hell.
My father preferred to wear some of his clothing back to front.
My father sends you this present of a large, almost sentient cheese.
My favourite day is always the second day of the year.
My first thought on discovering soldiers waiting in my sitting-room,
My first wife's ornament was almost the history of Latin America.
My first wife used to insult me far more ingeniously
My flag? Well, I think we can all guess what that looks like.
My friend, you very nearly produced something quite astonishingly
   good!
My genitalia seem strangely unreal tonight. Why is that?
My God, but how narrowly I missed being a failure!
My God, but these are terrible, terrible people!
My God, my God, what hast thou done with my foreskin?
My God, what an artist you were twenty-five years ago!
My grandparents fell to their death while attempting to have sex
My great-great-great-great-great-great-grandfather once spoke to
   Bolivar's secretary.
My head seems to be expanding and contracting
My heart aches, and a bout of uncontrollable farting noises
My heart aches, but her tiny underpants
My heart glows with the principles of integrity and truth;
My heart sinks right into my boots whenever I behold

My heart was beating wildly. But where on earth was the taxi?
My homeland is, essentially, early medieval
My hope was for a huge success – but without attracting much
    attention.
My inspiration has dried up at last (thank God!)
My intense passion for certain aspects of Far Eastern Culture
My life has been arranged by the stupidity of others.
My life has fallen apart, Eve.
My life's work, which I mean to tear up, if ever I can find the
    time,
My love is like a red, red wheelbarrow
My love, kindly do not point your sleeping eye
My love is somewhere in this gathering of 50,000 people.
My mother bored me terribly as a child;
My name is Death, since you ask. Now, *please*
My neighbour (whose name is the same as King Arthur's spear)
My own view is that Dame Juliana of Norwich would have shat
    herself
My private parts are not, I hope, excessively amusing.
My reasons for writing this are surely self-evident.
My remarks about the Jews were part of our own proud, ancient
    tradition.
My singing compatriots! Give loud praise for your local freedoms!
My son" – (the old man said) – "now with God, I'm afraid;
Mysticism, rather like a pain in the false teeth,
Mystics – those masturbators who mistake themselves for
    midwives –
My suggestion that the Buddha was probably Egyptian
Mythology is, basically, crap.
My thoughts are whirring about all over the place;
My too two tough limbs (Lord!) roughly together lashed
My whole life I have been struggling to keep my head above water.
My window shows the journeying underpants – erm –
My young son asks me, "Father? Why are you such a tosser?"
My youth was full of women whom I would gladly have begged

Nacrite, a clay mineral, identical in composition
Naked but for a charming little plastic crown of thorns,

"Naked women?" Whenever I hear the phrase,
Name me a single stupid Red Indian chieftain, I dare you.
Napier shall do what?
Naturally the Amazon rises in our homeland.
Nature came out of the closet and said to me: "Hello, gorgeous!"
Nature is probably God's sole mistake.
Nature is like a large ship in which three or four mischievous little
    beauties
Nay, rather stick thy thumb up thine own arse, My Lord,
Nearing the great historical site, we found we both needed a leak.
Nearly as tall as I am, but with a tiny front window,
Needless to say, as a middle-class white man,
Never again call me Norberto, Mother.
Never again to have any cause to return to that house!
Never in all my life have I seen such splendour!
Next year I hope to have a profoundly spiritual encounter
Next year I should have a good job in Addis Ababa.
Next year I too shall dope myself stupid in Afghanistan.
Nigel, when I heard that you had come back to life again,
No. Actually, I am not
No actual poem anywhere would begin like this
No ancient civilisation ever existed quite like that.
No ancient civilisation has ever existed quite like this.
No. A vast crowd never stood here, shrieking obscenities,
Nobody – but nobody – is ever really born again.
Nobody – but nobody – is interested in these flowers.
Nobody, I think, disputes the incredible beauty
No convert has any idea what his Church is really like.
No country whose name begins with a P will ever do anything
    worthwhile.
No. Do not visit Oblivia too early in your life;
No. Do not waste your time with what is merely real.
No. Fear not. I for one will never sell my birthright.
No great art has ever come from the Middle Classes.
No greater wisdom, surely, than to say this: If I
No great invention was ever made by a Protestant.
No. I am not afraid of a few billion madmen either.
No. I am not a nudist. However, if I were,
No! I am not in the slightest European.
No. I can no longer keep it a secret.

No, I do not think that folklore contains our deepest wisdom.
No. I did not abandon my inherited mansions.
No. I find mass murder simply unacceptable.
No. If it were not for the heart, it would be much colder.
No, I have certainly not had a reasonable life.
No, in my whole life, nothing so terrible
No. I refuse to compromise my art.
No; I shall never compare you to a randy mule.
No. It's no use. Why pretend any longer
No. It wasn't quite snowing.
No longer do I attempt to describe an entire universe
No longer do I even hear the strange screaming
No long perfection is possible, whether in art or in life;
No, Madam. Somebody else can climb to the top
No man has seen God at any time. No; nor woman neither.
No, Max. What you said was not entirely idiotic.
No more will we fart uncontrollably
No Moslem really believes that Jesus Christ was crucified.
No. My whole life has been spent struggling
None of the early centres of Christian Civilisation
None of these crosses have anything to do with Christianity.
None of us feel we have quite got deep enough into the Universe.
None of you people frighten me *in the f——ing slightest.*
No, never but by British feet
No, never but by British hips
No, never but by British knees
No, never but by *British* ships
Non-existent strong men are peculiarly empty
No! No disaster shall ever make my beloved Scotland land-locked.
No, no. It was only an apparent change, believe me.
No! Not another one being hurled over a precipice!
No. Not even death is harder than leaving this wondrous country.
No-one admires the moon more than I do myself;
No-one can prove that Jesus, Smith, or Mohammed
No-one can tell why Oscar Wilde was really arrested.
No-one denies that one or two of Einstein's wild guesses
No-one denies that the Universe is in extremely bad taste.
No-one ever objects to the noise a car makes here.
No-one has ever discovered any truth about a next world.
No-one has ever seen or heard or smelt God at any time.

No-one has ever written a poem quite like this before.
No-one has fought more justified Wars of Liberation
No-one is interested in reading about prostitutes;
No-one, it seems, gives a toss about the National Epic.
No-one measures Time. Time is itself the measurement.
No-one will ever be able to guess how it was done.
No-one will ever say of me: He couldn't even
No-one will ever suspect, not even remotely,
No real beach is ever as lonely as it pretends to be.
No, really. I'm all right. I've got at least two of them anyway.
No. Romantic Bolivia is not yet dead and gone.
North of the Andes, there is nothing of any interest;
No talk of failure! This time we must succeed.
Not all pilgrimages are a mere excuse for an orgy.
Not all the Saints were sociopathic, of course;
Not even death is harder than leaving Oblivia.
Not everything I say is overwhelmingly brilliant, I know.
No, thanks. I prefer to read what didn't happen in history.
No, that is no great secret. The dead have ceased to exist.
No. The arid rationalism of mere reality
No. There can never be a true Oblivian tyrant;
No, they are not angels. They are nudists.
Nothing has more pride in it than intense religious humility.
Nothing is a suggestion of the world to come.
Nothing is less beautiful than a doctor removing his shirt.
Nothing is more beautiful than a doctor removing her skirt.
Nothing later equalled that first distant glimpse
Nothingness? There is really no such thing.
Nothing that happens – nothing – can take away from me now
Nothing was heard of the absent man for almost fifty years;
Nothing whatever is going to stop us dying and disappearing.
No. This new version of the Mass with naked altar-boys
No. This sort of thing is not "absolutely normal".
Not in all those sunlit rooms, where widows are opening
Not literature? No? So what?
Not many people expect to die in a car-crash.
Not nonsense but the transcendence of mere earthly sense –
Not rarely has the thought of peaceful suicide
No true Bolivian has ever masturbated;
No true gentleman has an enormous backside;

No true Scot has ever died of a sexually transmitted disease.
No verbal brilliance, however exceptional, turns nonsense into truth.
Now, as the rest of the world looks on, while Oblivia
Now it's the turn of this generation to go to Hell as well.
Now, I would never suggest that anyone break the law –
Now, like a pervert with a lengthy elastic band,
No worthwhile human being has ever liked beer.
Now that age has delivered its traditional sedative,
Now that (at last!) I'm an old man wallowing in bitterness,
Now that Glasgow, with its magic carpets and jewelled pavements,
Now that I am too old to be called up for a war,
Now that I know everything, an inevitable whiff of boredom
Now that I know you are not just pretending to be a woman,
Now that Islam has managed to attract everyone else's attention,
Now that you are dead, and various ancient Israelites
Now the rest of Oblivia is asleep; but I sit here, holding
Not to have bailed out into fairy stories
"No. You just haven't done that right," Eve remarked.
Nude in Garnethill again, on a day of ridiculous warmth,

Oblivia! Home of so many ancient civilisations!
Oblivia! The slaves who urinated sadly in your jungles
Oblivia! With anguished gaze the entire universe looks on
Oblivia! With your innumerable and incomparable artists,
O Bolimia! Light-filled land full of laughing heterosexuals!
Obscurity, I find, has long been necessary for my peace of mind.
Observe this rare and precious object here.
Obviously, he was some sort of successful raider;
Obviously, no black woman
Obviously, not all foreigners are one hundred per cent perverts.
Obviously, one must have respect for people who threaten to kill
    you;
Obviously, said God, it is not something I am particularly proud of.
Obviously, we are very sorry that all those people were murdered.
Occasionally heads emerged from the enveloping mist.
O continent of three or four milliard virgins!
Odd, how utterly familiar her exotic foreign corner-cupboard was.
Odd, how utterly familiar her hot foreign harbour was!

Oddly enough, Britain had two King James the Firsts.
Oddly enough, my two favourite words are *clitoris* and *pederast*.
O exquisite Switzerland! Younger brother of Bolivia!
Of all the cities in present-day Oblivian lands
Of all the seasons it is the next one that I prefer most.
Of Bolivar and the South
Of Bolivia's future I make this loud, confident prophecy:
Of childhood, I remember little but some very strange clothing.
Of course! A huge great spot on my nose, on the very day
Of course, as a perverted foreign millionaire,
Of course a woman's underwear is more valuable than a man's
Of course, ducks should have equal opportunities
Of course, even the Yanqui is not to blame for absolutely everything.
Of course God created everything – in the very specialised sense
Of course, God's views on the foreskin demand our immense
    respect.
Of course I am not a genius. I am still alive, for one thing.
Of course I did not mean to scratch your perfect backside;
Of course, I did not use the word "prick" derogatively
Of course I do not suggest that the great if high-voiced prophet
Of course I don't hate *absolutely everybody*.
Of course I hate men. Doesn't everybody?
Of course I hate you. Who wouldn't?
Of course I'm a racist. Why else would I live with a ghost?
Of course I realise I am physically repulsive.
Of course, I take a close interest in literary failures.
Of course, it is not quite proven that, in Ancient Assyria,
Of course it is not the real Oblivia
Of course it was never my wish to fall right through the floor.
Of course, I was given the most flat-chested of the three
Of course, one does not deny that Homer had some talent.
Of course, one had long heard rumours that one might be going to
    die,
Of course, our land, more than any other land on earth,
Of course religious killing is not a form of murder;
Of course the dead are not around us themselves;
Of course there's a colour called topaz.
Of course, this is not really about Bilovia.
Of course, we regret the deaths. Particularly the children.
Of course we shall see this thing through to the bitter end.

Of course, when I killed that poor baby I was horrified.
Of course, when I lost control of the car and ploughed through a
    few dozen schoolchildren
Of course, when I ran that old cripple down I was mortified
Of course, when I ran those two old cripples down I was horrified
Of course, when the child fell off the window-sill again,
Of course you are not going to understand a single thing I say.
Off you go to the savage wilds of Uruguay,
Of *Man's* first – (F—— me rigid! What was that?)
Of Man's *second* disobedience, and the fart
Of Oblivia's future I make this cautious prophecy:
Of Oblivia's future I make this highly confident prophecy:
Of one thing we may be quite sure – that the Great Prophet never
    existed.
Often, to amuse themselves, sailors might nimbly pull down
Often, when reading Shakespeare, one finds oneself thinking:
    "Shit!
O God! Wonderful God! O, wonderful, wonderful God! One is
O great Bolivia, stern and wild!
Oh, all right maybe all my work is all useless after all.
Oh, all right. This habit of saying "eternal" for "infinite",
Oh, all talk of perfection is so much fatuity!
Oh, all ye trusty Oblivian sailors, come listen to me drone!
Oh, at last, at last – I'm losing the will to live!
"Oh, bleep!" said God, "I feel so deeply, deeply inadequate.
Oh, China! If it were not for Bolivia,
Oh, could I search the breasts of all those women upstairs,
Oh, Daddy, please tell us: What are you doing with our Aunt?
Oh, dear, dead saint, who bent over uncomplainingly
Oh, dear! St John has fallen down his ladder!
Oh, Earth! Like that first, uncontrollable spurt
Oh, everything looks quite interesting in the moonlight!
Oh, Father, pray tell me: What are you doing with the Cook?
Oh, for a thousand tongues with which to lick
Oh, for God's sake – not more bloody extraterrestrials!
Oh, for God's sake! Stop talking about the future, will you?
Oh, France! With your absurd conviction that France
"Oh fruck, no!" shrieked the Little Princess, with a gorgeous pout.
Oh, Germany! Almost none of these philosophers of yours
O God, do please forgive me for all my pre-ordained sins!

Oh, God – if I should ever finally lose interest in the monosyllable,
Oh God, I wish you would do that again but with your knickers off!
Oh, God! Morning again – and you still have the perfect
Oh, God – not another book about the never discussed!
Oh, God – not another book about the undiscussable!
Oh God, you know what it's like when you waken up and
Oh, go off and shit yourself at your Nobel Prize ceremony!
Oh, greater nothingness beyond mere nothingness!
Oh, Heat! Oh, thou which makest all things hot!
O, here comes Father McEvilly, that good and saintly man!
Oh, how I love being in the presence of a happy, knickerless saint!
Oh, how much I love Garamond question marks!
Oh, I admit your "Empress" is by no means the first prostitute
Oh, I dare say, if we were completely different
Oh, I dare say there are writers who do not have delusions of
    grandeur;
Oh, I don't doubt I may have made one or two little mistakes.
Oh, I don't worship anything – but, if I did,
Oh, if only my scrotum could whisper what I feel!
Oh, if only the Universe had been able to produce us too!
Oh, I lost my true love by laughing too loudly during her mother's
    funeral!
Oh, Indians, how could you break the nose of someone who loves
    you so much?
Oh, Intillimani, and the sudden glimpse of your fanny,
Oh, it was a jolly tinker and he fell over a cliff and died;
Oh, kindly cease to manipulate my private parts, Your Worship!
Oh, Kunst! What else is there to care about?
Oh, look! There's a wounded hare! Ha, ha, ha, ha!
Oh, Lord, I am your mount. Examine my teeth if you will,
Oh, love of God, surpassing sense and reason!
Oh Madam, the uncanny scent of that nearby factory
Oh, me auld Hielan mither had massive great tits;
Oh, my gorgeous little yellow-knickered beauty!
O Homeland! With cries of joy the civilised world looks on
Oh, our wonderful, troubled, depressed or drunken females!
Oh, Papa, do pray tell us: What are you doing with the new butler?
Oh, peace; oh, dove; oh loved one's flashes of temper;
Oh, please let the Universe be other than it is!
Oh, Schist! Oh, Schistosity! So little matters.

"Oh, shirt!" said God. "I've effing sent them all to the wrong place!"
Oh, soul of man! How very like a curt, all-promising fart
Oh stars! Oh buttons (one might say) on the divine long-johns!
Oh, surely a few thousand essentially innocent pleasures
Oh tedious, boring and mendacious whinger!
Oh, that old music again! Did I truly hear it?
Oh, the cry was "No more underpants!"
Oh, the delight of seeing you lift up your white dress!
Oh, the first time in a man's life when a lawyer sits on his head
Oh, to be in Oblivia, in any season at all!
Oh, well. Another morning, and still I have (or so I trust) a penis.
Oh, well. At least the Amazons didn't disfigure their buttocks.
Oh, whenever I think of the sea-coast of Oblivia,
Oh where, tell me where, has our much-beribboned Field Marshal
    gone?
Oh, which of us has ever been adequately appreciated?
Oh, why bother? What?
Oh, wonderful! Yet another golden-voiced nutcase!
"Oh, writer, what is it you do?" "I bounce beautiful balls."
Oh, youngest, best-loved daughter of Pachacútec Bloggis,
Oh, you powerful, attractive drugs, who can also talk!
Oh, you – the Stack Polly of World Literature!
Oh, you who are at the mercy of the depravity of tourists!
Oh you who are excited by the sight of the old dying!
Oh you, who dared to call Lenin "a turd if there ever was one" –
Oh you, who will pose in the nude on ruined altars, for dollars!
O, I am a spineless bastard-O
O, I come from the south of the north of the east of the nest in a
    vest,
O, I shall get to finger God's own goal
O, I wooed my true love in a local public convenience-O;
"Okay," said God, getting back up off the ground;
Old, I now find I am strangely proud of my collection of talking bras.
Old men talking through their arses is hardly wisdom as such, is it?
O Lord, Lord, Lord – I do not want the real world!
O Man, let me give you this important piece of advice:
O Man, put by your pride and listen to me!
O Moon! I'm afraid I'm not feeling terribly well.
O Mother Mary mild, from whose harmonic hoink
O My Homeland! With sheer disbelief the entire cosmos looks on

O, my swinging compatriots! I did warn you
O my underpants are like a red, red rose
On a dark night, unseen, in search of a good pull,
On any planet where Oblivia no longer existed
Once again, I took an astonishing risk!
Once his or her lover had gone out to kill themselves,
Once, I am sure, I could have nimbly climbed the balcony
Once more I say this to the United States of America:
Once more, O Muse, I am right in the mood for frenzied,
    mechanical sex.
Once more the Almighty intervened personally on my behalf,
Once more, the humiliation of feeling randy
Once one begins to realise how much more astute women can be
Once the ships have started sinking, the warning lights come on.
Once, while at an auction of Highly Important Watches,
One assumes that Saint John of the Cross was not much interested
    in schoolgirls.
One cannot pass one's entire life farting uncontrollably.
One cannot really imagine Wittgenstein wearing lederhosen
    comfortably;
One can predict the end of the world more or less for ever:
One could hardly run on the spot more brilliantly
One does not expect to hear an archangel being sick
One does not want to take all these dead soldiers too seriously.
One doesn't exactly think of God as being a *success*, does one?
One each, of course;
One feels that God might surely have made rather a better effort
One knows in one's heart that a bar called *The Giggling Inca*
One might sooner believe that Mozart died for our sins
One might think that Almighty God would find better things to do
One morning, as God was putting on a floral dress,
One morning, as I was washing a famous local pervert's windows,
One must remember, we are dealing with barbarians here.
One of my toenails hurts. But I suppose American history
One often feels that the human genitalia have been somewhat
    misdesigned;
One of the few things one knows for sure about the Unknowable
    is that
One of the levels of their Hell is, it seems, reserved entirely for
    Jews –

One or two moments in annihilation's glory;
One recorded crime outweighs a million unrecorded;
One screw is rarely quite enough –
One thing it is vitally important to know about life:
One thing is certain. There is no such thing as Destiny.
One tries not to think of Darwin with his penis out.
One would like to think it made determined strides impossible
One would not have minded making slightly more of a difference
On learning that his son and heir was, more accurately, his nephew,
Only a complete swine would write about these events
Only a great optimist would look to a University for bravery.
Only an old man talking quietly to himself in a burning field;
Only a single example of a heroic shit
Only for thee have I truly lived, O *Kunst*!
Only four people in the whole world know this language.
Only God can tell the sex of a child in the womb.
Only my compatriots know what sadness really is.
Only observe; the world is charged with its own grandeur;
Only one of the cases was related to the other.
Only very slowly did I gradually grasp
On second thoughts, *don't* follow me.
On that ferocious Alpine peak, *The Drooling Monk*,
On the bookcase, a gorgeous photo of you standing beside that
    same bookcase
On the first day of the new millennium, he discovered he had
    cancer.
On the wall, a heraldic sign with the words *PIGS FART*
On the whole, I am glad not to be somebody else.
On the whole, I care very little as to what is written about me.
On Thursday night, I did it again, I'm afraid.
Ooo arrr!
Or did I perhaps do something else?
Oscar Wilde, while on a railway journey from Jersey City,
O, Scotland! Though, perhaps, famed in none of the great arts,
O Señorita Parson! The sweet charms of thy person
O, that superb Bolivian metropolis on the seacoast,
Others fart uncontrollably. Thou art free.
O, thou! Deep inspiration of innumerable mammals!
O Thou whom Goethe called "the Great Englishman"!
O, Tracey said to Trevor: "Well, you know, this chap Pascal?

O truly astonishing product of the divine penis!
O Tupac Tuanga! Thud! It might well be said of you
O Tyrant Time, why must thou ever touch
Our ancestors – who couldn't bequeath us even a proper writing
   system –
Our hopes for a fairer world – and, of course, a larger Oblivia
Our journey ends just where so many think it is really starting;
Our peasants hardly know the meaning of the word "wifku".
Our Saviour, whose celebrated lack of interest in women
Our "true state" is evidently some ludicrous abstraction
Our very lives are Oblivian – austere, cool, yet caring;
Outgrow the sexual? What a superb idea!
Over the bent globe, the brilliant, bending authors
Over what but himself could God possibly be victorious?
O whistle and I'll fart uncontrollably, my lad;
O You who dared compare the Koran to a Fire Drill Poster!
O You who dared compare the Sacred Book to – well, to anything.
Ozone, an allotropic form of oxygen, present, some say,

Page after page after page after page about devils!
Paraguay! Your complete absence of mineral riches, alas,
Patriarchal Society! You are a very bad thing.
Patriarchal Society! You are a very, very bad thing.
Patriarchal Society! You are such a very, very bad thing indeed.
Peace to the onanist, whose morning glory
People waiting for long days in the spaces
Perfection is hardly a realistic option, is it?
Perhaps, at this very moment you are sitting in Paris, fondling
Perhaps a vast crowd once stood here, shrieking obscenities.
Perhaps I am the biggest hypocrite of the lot.
Perhaps I have had my fill of beautiful loonies by now.
Perhaps I have not been the perfect son of Oblivia;
Perhaps I have risen too far above the disgusting vulgarity
Perhaps I have *too much* in common with Almighty God.
Perhaps in some technical sense I am indeed invisible?
Perhaps I should have done less
Perhaps I should have done more
Perhaps I should have done much the same

Perhaps I should not have stood at my study window, pointing
Perhaps it is merely my excessive perfectionism
Perhaps it's just as well I didn't
Perhaps, Jeff, you are not *bad enough* to win the Nobel Prize?
Perhaps only God can make a really good cup of tea.
Perhaps political cretinism is roughly the general norm.
"Perhaps," said God, "I should have made a bit more of an effort."
Perhaps the great age of the Irish slave-raids
Perhaps to some, 30,000 lines about obsolete weaponry
Perhaps we are the morning sickness of the world;
Perhaps you wish to know my views about female psychology?
Personally, I find Goneril and Regan massively attractive. (And so
   feminine!)
Personally I find the man rather irritating.
Personally I find the sun rather irritating
Personally, I regard most animals as absurd.
Personally, I regard the Sun as a bit of a failure.
Personally, I suspect God moves the stars by surreptitious farting.
Personally, I think an eternity of looking respectfully at beavers
Personally, I think high temperature is grossly over-rated.
Personally, I think Mount Fuji is quite the wrong shape.
Personally, I think the whole bloody universe is the wrong shape.
Personally, I would have killed Scheherazade somewhere about
   Night Sixty.
Peru! Let us by all means be completely honest for a moment.
Pessoa! Fool! I have now lived for far longer than you ever did.
Pissing against a wall as a second funeral came round the corner,
Piss off. Of course women are more beautiful than men.
Pius the Ninth (a saint) used to let a little boy
Pizarro's rank stink floats ignobly through the great columns
Playing games is precisely what I am not doing.
Please don't ignore me, whatever you do!
Please don't take me back to that bloody place again!
Please ignore me.
Please ignore me completely.
Please ignore me now and again.
Please let me know, now and then, how you are doing;
Please let me know, now and then, how your leg is doing;
Please make the taxman die, oh dear Saint Jude!
Please move that jamjar further from my bed. Thank you.

Please, please give me several thousand dollars now!
Please send me a cheque for a large amount of money.
Poet! Tell the people to go and —— themselves!
Political cretinism is the norm for creative artist.
Ponce! There! Ponce! The truth is out at last!
Poor, miserable beggar girl, whose tiny, tedious breasts
Popes have been evil. So what? This in no way affects
Possibly there is some value in what I write;
Possibly there is no value in what I write;
Professor? Why are there shit marks on the ceiling of your fine
    office?
Protect me from flies, dust, and the forces of evil!
Proud maiden! Can you not even smile while you undress
Proud maiden! The unforgiveable social forces
Proud maiden! The unforgiving social forces which compel me
Proust did not think of himself as a rich man.
Proust! I feel no desire to learn more about your gropings
Proust! I have now lived for far longer than you ever did.
Proust is, quite simply, even better than the Gospels, Pal.
Prove to me if you can, you smirking fools, that Jesus really died!

Quechua is spoken in all my dreams, except when
Quite frankly, I don't like the way you people smile.
Quite frankly, the world has irritated the bejebus out of me.
Quite simply, there is no such thing as Divine Revelation.
Quite suddenly, I am tired even of that cloth which

Rain. Rain. Rain. Rain. Raisins. What? Raining again?
Rapt as I was in a volume of Pythagoras in Old Cymric,
Rarely can there have been a better time to be dead!
Rather than lose a tooth, he chose to kill himself.
Rather than take all her clothes off, she admitted she was guilty;
Reading about Bannockburn, one pretty well always thinks
Reading Kafu in Arabic in my second home in Provence,
Reality is rather inadequate for the likes of us.
Really I am being kept quite extraordinarily busy;

Really, in the end, what it all boils down to
Really, it is not quite for me to switch your light on and off.
Reasonable criticism is one thing. But cheap sneers
Recent evidence that Napoleon was of Bolivian descent
Relieving myself in the wild Andean valleys,
Religion and profound thought are hardly compatible;
Religion has a very great deal to do with making a living.
Religion (in an even deeper sense of the term)
Religion (in the deepest sense of the term)
Religion is far greater than mere moral decency;
Religion is the surest foundation of the immoral life.
Religious behaviour – in fact, neurotic behaviour in general –
Religious symbolism is pretty well never valuable.
Reluctant though I am to leave you in this,
Rembrandt? Yes. I have certainly heard the name mentioned.
Remember how, on that day when you were ill,
Remember that time you gasped: "What a gloriously tooled cock!"
"Respect me or I'll kill you"? Hmm. A powerful argument,
    certainly.
Returning home, expecting a hero's welcome,
Returning to La Paz after a long, unintended exile
Right. Let's get into the classic position.
Right, Matey. It's time to tell the Truth to Power.
Right. Never again shall I put up with something like this.
"Right," said Job. "That's it. That is absolutely the last effing straw.
Rilke was, basically, an astrologer.
Robert Burns? The name rings a vague bell.
Roman Catholicism is a children's game of importance.
Roman literature is by and large dreadful, is it not?
Romeo and Juliet is, essentially, a pederastic fantasy.
Round the back of the church, where the drunken priests like to
    sleep,
Round the bend, Mate? *Moi*?

Sacred texts are, essentially, a sort of crossword puzzle.
Sad, chastened, he pocketed the six million
Said God: "But I am so much more wonderful than that!
Saint Augustine was clearly one of the great bores of all time.

Saint Patrick – a classic British religious maniac –
Saucer! For a long time I have found immense significance
Sausages and options, and that big bed in the bay-window –
Scarcely anyone has really seen Oblivia before,
Science, as Blake understood, is the only true religion.
Science – Enlightenment – Compassion – not to mention
    Obscenity –
Scotland! Dark country, full of homosexuals!
Scotland! Our European idiot brother!
Secure in our little boxes, thundering over Niagara,
Seduced though I rarely am by the wild applause of my public,
Seeing, hearing, talking, touching, falling,
Señora Realli, I wonder if you would mind me asking,
Set free all the prisoners again!
Setting decent old people on fire for a grossly inadequate reason
Sexual activity is, ultimately, for failures;
Shakespeare? I confess the name is not wholly unfamiliar to me.
Shakespeare! My wild half-brother!
Shakespeare, Proust, Tao Yuan-Ming, the *Thousand and One Nights*,
Shall I ever forget that moment when I first realised
Shall I never again see the Lesser Hu'ugstu'ndleireu Hills?
Shall there come a time when even my feelings for you
Sharp Death shall hash no living shufti
Shattered by the uncanny power of Gogol's *Lower Depths*,
She certainly behaves like someone who knows what she knows.
She'll get sick of the whole business soon enough, I thought.
She said: "It's a two-thousand-year-old toilet seat."
She sat with her back to the huge big corner window;
She's the female equivalent of all those poisoned dwarves
She stood beside the bed, laughing hilariously.
She told us an utterly amazing story. She said
She took me into the dull office and showed me her little baps;
Shitting oneself for fear is hardly the heroic gesture
Shooting priests is always, in the long run, a mistake;
Short legs, and no backside at all? Hmm. Tricky.
Shortly after the Mongols had conquered the whole of China,
Shove your latest brilliant haiku up your backside, Dear Master.
Showing off the lovely old thing to me in the bathroom,
Shug MacRobbie! You're a poet! (Several of them, in fact.)
Siberia! At least you are the right size for a poet!

Sibylla! At least thou art the right size for a poet like me!
Silence, as Black remarked, is the only true religion.
Silence, deplorable poof!
Simultaneously phobic in thirteen different directions,
Since Almighty God has asked me to try to prevent people
Since, fortunately, I had no choice between
Since God is gay, said the New Prophet, that is good enough for
    me.
Since God is impossible, small wonder we are at such a loss
Since God is not there, it must always be something else
Since he does not exist, of course he is invisible.
Since he laughed at whatever he did not understand, he was
    forever laughing;
Since he who made heaven made earth, and earth is no joke,
Since I am on this side of it, not on that side of it,
Since I am relentlessly opposed to all the bourgeois values,
Since I at best have only an hour or two of life left,
Since I have somehow managed to reach a superhuman level
Since it is predestined that I will write this poem,
Since I, who have a Greek Dog's body,
Since me a many with light the Lord God (flashing) favoured have
Since my father's name is Leo, it is I suppose appropriate
Since the President's moustache is more important than the Andes,
Since the probability of this God is inherently zero,
Since we cannot be content that things are what they are,
Since what gets named as God is always *something else*,
Sing, Muse, of the quite startling amount of underpants
Sing on and dance in the chains of tyranny!
Sin is not always the high road to virtue;
Sir! A perverted ghost has stolen my income-tax forms!
Sir Francis, your hell-inspired ingenuity and Satanic hatred
Sir, isn't your wife a man? Did she really produce children?
Sir, surely a few dozen uninhibited photographs of your daughter
Sir, when I said that nothing from your pen could be tedious,
Sitting by an old lady at dinner in Coquimbo,
Sitting dead in front of the television,
"Sitting in my father's library there is an astonishing giant,
Sitting in the kitchen, with her tiny tits out, an absent-minded aunt
    of mine
Six o'clock. Shit! What am I lying on top of now?

Slay those who refuse to believe in the God of Mercy!
Smith! Lifelong student of literature and the fine arts!
Smug, stunted fool, who asks of the Gospel: "But is it *true*?"
Snow?
Snow! If I
So Abraham went back down the hill, carrying his son's small
    testicles,
So, Cardinal. Time to "develop" another unchangeable truth, is it?
So here I am, an old fool who still worships doughnuts;
So. Here we are in a world where people really do speak Baltic
So. How many cars have travelled on the earth by now, do you
    think?
So I simply flung on the first veil I could find
So long as my children are healthy, sane and Oblivian,
Someone at the window – though I could not quite see who –
Someone is playing a guitar at five in the morning.
Someone keeps frightening the nearby giraffes every night.
Someone with a socket is clearly more important
Some say the world will end with a loud flatulent rip;
Something about real people irritates me profoundly;
Something amazing happened to me last night.
Something dropped me down into the Moon's cold palace
Something rather interesting is wrong with my urine today.
Some things are more important than the truth, Simon.
Some things are the result of divine intervention;
Some think the world will end in a plague of misprints;
Sometimes God loves a people so much he completely wipes them
    out.
Sometimes I just suddenly burst out weeping, for no good reason.
Sometimes it seems there is a ghostly tool in the clouds
Somewhere deep in the fabric of my being
Somewhere down a dark lane, a voice cries out for Jesus.
So, Moses. What's been happening in the world of literature?
So much can seduce me from going to the Shakespearean brothel.
So much can tempt me from my study of Bolivian folk crafts;
So much coast on this vast continent! How can none of it
So much depends on the proper mistranslation;
So much joy, so much pain, so much boredom,
So much of astronomy seems to *exaggerate* terribly.
So much of my life has been decorated by busts,

So much pain, so much joy, so much bad food,

So much that seemed original to oneself

Soon we'll all be dead, and we won't have to read the scriptures

So strange now, to think I once shat myself in Shiraz;

So there I was in the cab, with Pushkin and Griboyedov,

So there we are. Billions stunned by imaginary details

So. There we were all relieving ourselves halfway up the Andes.

So. To the stars even the Great Divide must seem more or less
    nothing.

So. What was the religion in Jerusalem

So. Why am I sitting here?

Speaking as a fantastic genetic freak,

Speak not so much, I beg you, of my wise and tolerant
    compassion,

Spending all night in the public lavatories, Baldwin,

Spending thirty-three years in prison for a crime one did not
    commit

Spending twenty-six years in prison for a crime one does not
    remember committing,

Spices from all over the world I add to my Oblivian stew.

Spring again! And how insufferably tedious

Spring again! – and the desire to poke away at local shop assistants

Standing in the kitchen, with her tiny self-conscious tits out

Standing rather self-consciously at the front door, the triplets

Stop, Passer-by! No – Stop, I beg thee! Stop! Please stop!

Stepping late one night out of the *Dr Francia y Don José*,

Strange how so often it is the wrong buildings which fall down.

Striding about your flat in the buff while you were out

Stuck down here among all the bloody *animals*!

Submit to the Inevitable? What else can one do to the Inevitable?

Such as have gently entertained themselves behind a church at dusk

Such a tragedy that someone didn't shoot the man sooner!

Suddenly, an explosion ripped through the Universe!

Suddenly, an explosion rocked the house –

Suddenly he dropped dead of erectile dysfunction.

Suddenly, I came back to consciousness. Oh, no! No!

Suddenly I have become quite interested in Bylivia.

Suddenly I realised I had no idea where I was.

Suddenly I realised why the house seemed so familiar.

Suddenly, it is almost as if in some way I am old.

Suddenly, it occurred to me to look under the bed.
Suddenly I was woken up by my own sobbing.
Suddenly people started dropping dead in Heaven.
Suddenly she fell to the floor, dead. Or so we assumed.
Suddenly the corpse sighed: Oh God, I think that was it!
Suddenly the Pope's corpse, as it were, exploded.
Surely a minor weakness for untruthfulness
Surely a permanent world would be even worse. No?
Surely it is generally accepted by now that we are incomparable?
Surely it is high time for a good clear-out
Surely it's as much a novel as anything else?
Surely John Paul the Second and the Ayatollah Khomeini
Surely Lewis Carroll wasn't a poofter as well?
Surely only an Oblivian could ever understand
Surely this large fresco of *Pontius Pilate Washing His Hair*
Surely we are shortly to enter the Oblivian century?
Surprised by the urgent need to release some wind in an airport,
Sweet Jesus Christ, who should have invented the telephone

Take care, friend, not to be too 'factual' about religion;
Take care to obey the almighty, all-arranging sustainer
Take care you do not piss in the wrong direction.
Take care you do not pray in the wrong direction,
Take women's advice, said Omar, then do the opposite.
Talking to animals can be such a waste of time.
Talking with eighty-five thousand people on Fair Isle the other day,
Tell me something. Wasn't Martin Luther a Catholic for longer
Tell the cups what they want to hear. "Real life starts when you've
    been shattered.
Thank God, all the erections of the previous century
Thank God we don't see a zillionth of all the sexual activity
Thank you for blowing up the Parthenon again.
Thank you for the grace with which you suggest I am a liar;
Thank you, Professor, for showing off to me in your underwear.
Thank you so much, O Universe, for making me the sole exception
Thank you, Saint Jude! My penis no longer seeps pus.
Thank you, Spain, for not killing all of us.
That beautiful Indian often on the balcony opposite

That boxer who turned to religion, then gnawed his opponent's
    head off,
That fervour-favour, ah, the raving fever
That glorious Easter Day the members rose from the dead!
That halfwit Homer, who, as Petrarch observed,
That halfwit Petrarch, who, as Montaigne observed,
That long day when we sat out on the balcony together
That most of the Ancient Greeks were enthusiastic pederasts
That picture of God's great-great-grandmother above her bed
That Queen Victoria had an orgasm in Fingal's Cave
That Queen Victoria had an orgasm on Iona
That Queen Victoria had an orgasm while rounding the Mull of
    Kintyre,
That Queen Victoria might never have had an orgasm in her entire
    life
That sense of a vague permanent appointment with a Dentist up
    ahead:
That sound of squeaking immediately overhead
That strange hole which lately opened up in the fabric of Time
That surely must have been a most satisfying trip
That talking which lasted all night, and made the night seem short,
That that that that that that that that that that – and this –
That the Holy Father slipped suddenly from the balcony
That we somehow live on after we have ceased to function
That which starts movement going must already have been in
    motion.
That your parents were obviously the sacred gerbils
The absolute *All-That-Exists* is full of something else.
The altered look of these ancient mountainside altars
The ancient sage, having shat himself in private,
The Andes and its rivers ignore our changing borders;
The anoraks of Time invariably possess hoods, Hank.
The answer, my friend, is a resonant but ultimately empty phrase;
The appalling crimes which prove that God is looking after His
    Church
The appalling smell which now emanates from my beloved's body
The apparition of labia in the clouds – a saint's, presumably? –
The astonishing level of public interest in my work
The baby gave a soft, almost inaudible gasp,
The backside of the Universe is far too big.

The belief that a heap of crap shall be reanimated
The best religion is a form of grief
The chances that the Prophet is actually entombed there
The children selling themselves at the back of the great cathedral
   here
The child screaming with earache proclaims the glory of God;
The clouds piled up grey over West Graham Street.
The confusion of fact and fiction lies at the heart
The Cosmos came about through God's quite astonishing vanity;
The Crucifixion was essentially a private tragedy.
The day after most people leave, a letter arrives
The day grows dull, and I am still a pervert.
The days of glory have, as usual, departed.
The dead are dead are dead are dead
The dead are dead are dear are deaf
The dead are from time to time only pretending to be dead –
The desire to dance naked in a presumably disused abattoir
The discovery that God actually was a fish
The dominant note is surely one of exasperation
The duty of the true believer to kill other misguided people
The Emperor himself told me he had nothing but admiration
The entire universe is a sort of clerical error;
The entire world is a dream which no-one had.
The essential courage and nobility of male mendacity
The eternal comings and goings of important men
The eternal comings and goings of impotent men
The eternal question of Oblivian nationality
The ever-growing awareness that one is, technically, an idiot
The evidence that, in ancient times, it was the Bolivian indigene
The fact that we really die rules all this nonsense out;
The fart that once through Tartan Halls
The fiery red hair of the typical Ancient Egyptian
The first, infantile scream of any of the great musicians
The first inhabitants of this land were a few shameless perverts;
The first signs of the illness which eventually killed me
The first thing I knew was, someone had kicked the door in.
The first thing we do, let's close down all the Literature
   Departments,
The first time I stepped over a dead body in the street,
The first tweaks of what will be one's fatal illness

The flush flashed crash, fire skies! Dint (hymn him!) cross crust(ed)
   Christ –
The fool has said in his heart there is no go
The fool has said in his heart: There is no Goy
The fool hath said in his heart: There is no Goa.
The fool who persists in his mistranslations shall become canonical;
The full truth is rarely consonant with family feelings.
The full truth? Well, it's a target, I suppose.
The future of all art is surely Oblivian.
The general ugliness of the human male
The God of Moses is obviously named after Jove;
The Gods of this location were never seen without hats.
The Good Lord creates you either one way or the other;
The Governor himself told me he had nothing but admiration
The great Bolivian inventors of the aeroplane
The great freedom-fighter's son does seem, er, somewhat *fragrant*;
The Great Inca sits in Cuzco Town, drinking the blood-red wine.
The great novelists were, in their various great ways, fools;
The great, 600-metre long monster of Titicaca
The growing apprehension one feels about one's underwear
The heavens proclaim, if anything, the glory of the heavens;
The heavens proclaim nothing, Victor. Absolutely nothing.
The highest wisdom consists in not blaming the Highest Authority.
The high-hung balls in clouds, which goad good Christ, my gaud,
The history of any decent-sized hotel
The human mind's capacity for pattern recognition
The human mind's capacity for self-deception
The "human side of religion" is religion.
The idea that the universe is ruled by bribery
The Incarnation is a complex fiction, Vince.
The incredible number of shits that visit our country,
The Ineffable requires males to have their foreskins removed;
The infinite variety of purse-driven behaviour
The Japanese (who, it seems, migrated in from Korea)
The Jews were not an especially monotheistic people;
The King went out to hunt, but fell through a hole in the earth.
The lapering shchiumach lairts the haery plunnet, Sir Aleck.
The largest internal drainage system in South America
The last millennium was largely a mistake, I suspect.
The last rays of the sun lit up the disgusting face

The last thing I want to do is awaken interest
The latex of all the world is hot for me.
The laughing womb – or perhaps I should say, rather,
The leaves fell; and so did I. Though less elegantly.
The lecherous foreigner, crazed with lust for our women,
The Life of Mohammed is the world of the *Arabian Nights*.
The Lord started to take all his clothes off.
The lunatic, the lover and the Bolivian,
The magnificence of Spring slowly climbs into the pockets
The magnificent way in which we handed over so much
The main difference between you and me, my darling,
The main problem is simply that I now know so very much more
The man in the seat in front of us was just beginning to go bald,
The matadors of Iona are all incredible cowards.
The matadors of Ionia have gone off somewhere else.
The men who wrote these scriptures had a weakness for certain
    numbers;
The mere sight of that nameplate which said *Wufka*
The moment before you were conceived, you were nowhere at all;
The moon has never had a single emotion in its entire life.
The moon is not sad at present; for it can see Oblivia.
The moon is surely an unusual shape tonight?
The more I learn about women the less I seem to know
The most important thing, Genghis, is to behave decently.
The mournful sound of neighbours pissing in their gardens
The moving penis dribbles and, having dribbled,
The murderous foreign press of course makes much of a few deaths
Then came that dreadful day when a divine testicle exploded;
The newly discovered, steamily erotic diary of Walter Scott
The news that Pablo Neruda was in fact an FBI agent
The night would be very quiet, did I not fart so frequently;
The nocturnal emissions which are life are slowly changing
The noise of fairies mating in a nearby public park
The Non-Existent has never let us down before, has it?
Then, quite suddenly, we realised the theatre was completely useless.
The Oblivian flag, most beautiful in the whole world,
The obvious capital city for all of South America
The oilèd eyelid ails the soiled (wh)eel of light
The old have been around for somewhat longer than the young.
The old woman with her hair cut straight across her forehead

The Omnipotent hates evil – but somehow it happens anyway.
The Omnipresent must inhabit every rape and murder too. No?
The only thing I'd do different is, I'd talk to people more.
The only thing I seem to have inherited from my father
The passage of time must render all our masterpieces ludicrous.
The past is less important than my post
The past? No. I wish I knew what the *present* is like.
The people who own our Highlands are largely sexual perverts.
The Perfect Man has better things to do than read Scriptures.
The perpetual adoration of the Blessed Virgin's grotto
The physical extermination of most of the lowland tribes
The physicality which "obstructs" us is what we actually are.
The picturesque hopelessness of this place greatly reminds me
The poet loads himself with golden chains then tries to escape
    (nearly always unsuccessfully).
The present Pope clearly does not think very much of women.
The priest first had his fingers smashed with a mallet
The priest had first smashed his fingers with a mallet
The profoundest love more or less cries out to be punished;
The proper method to improve our manner of warming
The proper method to improve our manner of worming
The proper response to most of these beliefs is honest laughter.
The prospect of being dead interested her strangely;
The public hissteria provoked by my latest work
The question is, why are some of us not obsessed by bores?
The question of whether a black cat is even more beautiful
The quintessentially Celtic fascination with whelks
The Real God has never given anything in writing to anybody.
The real universe is no longer here any more.
There are at least eleven female qualities which
There are more important things than freedom, tolerance, reason;
There are no atheists on this continent.
There are no other writers
There are not a few great writers whom the world is worse off for
    having.
There are, of course, no truly honest church attendants.
There are so many days on which I do not die.
There are some astonishing similarities
There are some eight or nine women whom I think of very often.
There are things one would rather die than have found out.

There are times when I feel I would like to go back to Haparanda.
There are times when I feel I would like to go back to Khatanga.
There are times when I find it difficult to restrain myself
The reason why I prefer to have sex with stupid foreigners
There can be no such thing as an eternal passion.
There can be no true Bolivian who does not wholly agree with me
The recent claim of China to the so-called "Falkland Islands"
The recent sexed-up version of the Koran
There comes a time when jokes about lethal sexual diseases
The refusal to accept death for what it so obviously is
There is absolutely nothing I wish to say about poetry.
There is almost no excuse for writing comedies.
There is also enough light in the Universe already
There is always at least something to be said for telling the truth,
    Verity.
There is certainly no shortage of Gods in the Bible.
There is enough darkness in the Universe already.
There is far too much needing done in this bloody hall.
"There is far too much needing to be done on this effing planet!"
There is more mystery in any actual curtain
There is nearly always something better to do
There is no excuse whatsoever for writing tragedies.
There is no-one else in this building, Madam, whom I would
    rather do business with
There is no substitute for doing the hard work – [All the great
    creative figures are the same in that]
There is no substitute for doing the hard work – [Except perhaps
    getting other people to do it for you.]
There is no such thing as a being of a higher order –
There is no such thing as advanced religious thought;
There is no such thing as a genuine mystical insight.
There is no such thing as an actual message from the beyond.
There is no such thing as an eternal beam
There is no such thing as an eternal spring.
There is no such thing as an infinite experience
There is no such thing as an infinite sensibility.
There is no such thing as an Oblivian weed;
There is no such thing as a parallel supernatural world
There is no such thing as infinite wisdom – or, for that matter,
There is no such thing as non-material beauty;

There is no such thing as the Collective Unconscious.
There is no such thing as visionary truth.
There is no such thing as Zeno's Paradox, if we mean
There is nothing beyond
There is nothing else that I would more like to do
There is only one imperial city. There is only one La Paz.
There is only one poem which I really regret writing;
There is only one reason why people really do anything.
There is only one sure remedy for restive, murmuring workers.
There is something about this rain which does not quite convince me
There is something essentially dishonest about heterosexuality.
There is something exquisitely right about Bolivian rain and mud.
There is something faintly obscene about the entire Universe.
There is something not unamusing in the deaths of fairly remote
  relatives
There is something profoundly erotic about archaeological digs.
There is something profoundly erotic about undeserved failure.
  Isn't there?
There is something strangely sexy about extinction.
There is something terribly common about trying to save the
  Universe.
There is something terribly second-rate about death.
There is something terribly uninteresting about immortality. Isn't
  there
There is something terribly unprofound about making sense.
There is surely something slightly unnatural about children.
There I stood, holding a dead body, perhaps shouting
The religious inability to tell truth from fable
There's a great deal of it I miss, Anlivia,
There shall never come a time when my feelings for you will cool
There's something not quite convincing about it, isn't there?
The rest of Oblivia is asleep; while I sit here, waving
There was a nun sitting in the corner!
There was a nurse sitting in the other corner!
There was a sort of shed round at the back of the house
There was a time when *chaco, col* and *yunga*
There was a time when meadows, streams and warm crannies
There was no-one else anywhere in the whole room!
There was once in Annan a Nazi, a Wali, a Kazi and a Wazir;
There were so many days on which I did not die.

There were two young Bolivians – one of whom (myself in fact)
There will never come a time when my feelings for you shall cool
The river walked up to me, coughed and said: "Listen, Mate.
The rock, the red, the rid, the randy
The sacralisation of confusion and obtuseness
The sad fact is: they really are all doing the best they can.
The sad truth is that Socrates was just asking for it.
The scars have returned (which were invisible yesterday)
The scientist dares to tell us that butterflies are insects!
The sea is extremely turbulent tonight *again.*
The sea just is. The sea just happens to be. [But do I just happen to
    be walking along beside it?]
The sea just is. The sea just happens to be. [Of course, one may say
    the same about anything else;]
These are almost the very same underpants I wore when
These biographies all have so much space for minor, walk-on parts.
These days I fart too much to be quite sure what love really is.
These days I have to force myself to be charming.
These days only perverts ride horses.
These dreams of permanence are the worst of the world's delusions.
These fifteen thousand lines about your dead mother's buns
These fools who suppose than an obscure, long-dead criminal
These inescapable delusions that you have somehow seen through
These magnificent rainbow arcs of mystic bubble
These months of diarrhoea, by means of which God is testing me
These mountains are like my wife's sighing in the early dawn.
These mystical dreams I have, O Lenin, of smearing myself with
    your excrement,
These not quite thinkable, not yet sayable, but very fashionable
    thoughts
The sense that one spends one's whole life struggling uphill
These things are the dregs of paganism;
These young priests, who hang around the sacristies, saying
The sheer amount that seems to happen *to other bloody people*!
The shop-girl who sold me this knife had a fantastic frying pan
The sight of my translator's delightful tight little gate
The silent telephone threatens me day after day.
The simple fact is that God must be predestined too.
The simple truth is, I have just so much to spare.
The six nuns shrieked with fear and spread their rank terror

The soul, not existing, is superbly adapted for hiding.
The spiritual is a material fantasy;
The spiritual is the refusal to take the inanimate seriously.
The spiritual trance is a form of self-abuse.
The spiritual world is the world of self-flattery.
The statues in the cemeteries all began to sprout
The street, abandoned but for two or three monks,
The street, abandoned but for two or three hundred prostitutes,
The striking view that, after one has ceased to exist,
The struggle to play a decent game with what you have been dealt
The sudden fart of some mysterious ghost
The sun has gone down behind lofty Illampù
The Sun is God. Or it would be, if it didn't exist.
The sun itself thrusts its mighty penis through your bedroom
    window.
The tagged man lay dead for seven years – but then
The taking of Christ's name in vain *is* Christianity.
The tortured figure farting on the scaffold
The tragedy of life is that – er – you might say
The transcendental transcends even existence.
The traitors who introduced the new religion here
The trembling knees of the people in the Temple
The tremendous guilt I carry for being a white, heterosexual male
The true Bolivian has musculature like steel;
The true life depends upon delusions of grandeur;
The True Prophet asks for money so winningly
The true religion consists in doing what you have to do anyway.
The truly great man knows how to talk to invertebrates.
The "Twaj Mahal"? Hmm. A strangely convincing misprint.
The twelve pillars on the mountain, a single one for each
The typical saint is a boring, self-obsessed fool. No?
The typical spleen and bluster of the ideological mind
"The unacceptable vulgarity of the death threat" *(Auden)*
The undoubted fact that this Great Man never shat or masturbated
THE UNIVERSE CERTAINLY CANNOT REMEMBER
    ITSELF.
The universe does not have a secret purpose.
The Universe doesn't quite have the ring of truth about it.
The universe is a rather fine bit of local colour
The universe is a single giant symbol

The Universe is not quite up to standard, is it?
The Universe is something of a private tragedy.
The Universe is very very big.
The universe no doubt must have seemed rather a good idea at the
    time;
The universe, of course, must come from somewhere else.
The various spiritual suppositories
The Vatican seems to be terribly short of blamph
The veneration of scripture looks to literature for too much;
The very shy parish priest stopped playing with the children
The view that Israel was once to be found in God's bowels
The view that Mohammed was perhaps some sort of Jew
The view that the Buddha was, in fact, a criminal
The view that the Byzantines eked out the sacred incense with
    priestly dung
The view that we have three, four or perhaps five souls
The wall falls down, and a figure in the smoke
The wan white buttocks of the deserted heroine
The warmth. The naked woman. The open door. The flag.
The way they gently sag to the side there, for instance,
The whole world is the Man in the Iron Mask.
The whole world seems to be manipulating its private parts
The wild wind which, as usual, is saying nothing,
The wise view that Peru is a land of extra-terrestrials
The word 'God' is a barrier to understanding the real world.
The word 'God' is among the strongest of blasphemies, Rae.
The word 'Oblivian' and the word 'Civilisation'
The world as a sort of act of divine masturbation
The world is a book which some bad-mannered God has torn
    pages out of;
The world is as much about Leonardo's bacteria
The world is full of empty and meaningless erections
The world is full of nice people not doing their job;
The world is full of people who would like to sleep.
The world is full of the grandeur of failed priests.
The world is no illusion. It just feels like it sometimes.
The world is *not* charged with the glory of God, actually.
The world is suffused with imaginary gods.
They are all living in the houses I should be living in!
They are not long, the days of farting uncontrollably;

They do not seem to realise how my love
They do still sell books somewhere in this country, don't they?
They floated down the sewers, talking about great things;
They gazed on their Lord's face; and then ate, drank and farted,
They have all gone into a world of uncontrollable farting noises;
The young thug laboriously kicking a hedge outside our patio
They say the llama and alpaca keep
They've given him the Nobel Prize for the wrong bloody subject!
They were perverts, most of the saints, or perhaps never existed,
Thinke not, *Belinda*, that thy *Bumme*
Thinking of nothing but their vows that they would crush the
    Paraguayans,
Thinking of the beams of Bolivia's light-houses,
Thinking of the stairways of Oblivia's great homes,
Thirty years after he chucked himself out of a window,
This above all it is my duty to tell you.
This ancient pullover of mine which you once wore
This beating in one's head, which some call, God;
This Bolivia never did, nor never shall
This *Book of Odes* is surely to a large extent crap?
This city should really be ours, you know; not yours.
This comic operetta with real corpses
This computer-generated picture of 'Bible John''s knees
This country, being almost nowhere, is everywhere.
This country could well be called God's shaving brush,
This disgusting bias in favour of the real
This eastern wind has blown for the last five years.
This eerie sense sometimes that they are all the same person
This empty stairway, where I was once overpowered
This endless idealisation of some tart or other
This endless piffle about an ancient rabbit
This habit of saying "infinite" for "eternal"
This huge stain that goes shooting through my skull
This is a bloody useless language, is it not?
This is all so terribly unnecessary.
This is a terrible city. I hope everyone here
"This is my beloved son. Don't trust him an inch,"
This is, of course, an appalling thing to admit – but
This is the dawning of the Age of Irresponsible Farting Noises;
This is the very spot where the old Prince buried his toy soldiers.

This is the very spot where the young Prince buried his severed leg.

This lonely slope behind the nunnery has always been very dear to me;

This mental illness which supposes itself to be the height of profound insight

This message from the Beyond reads: *Where the Hell are we?*

This morning, while I was having a quiet snooze in the church,

This new Pope looks even more like a chronic masturbator

This person walking confidently up the road towards me

This Shakespeare seems to have been quite remarkably bald.

This statue of a bigot and a paedophile

This, thought God, could turn out to be a *lot* of trouble for nothing.

This time, O Balivia, it is definitely going to be different!

This tin can is my favourite model of the universe.

This trick of mistaking everything for an invisible person

This universe of darkness, punctuated by idiots,

This whole place is a navigational error.

This wonderful symbol, which symbolises another wonderful symbol,

This world is a sunlit porch in front of a slaughter-house;

This world is the filthiest part of God;

Thomas Campbell, not perhaps the greatest of English poets,

Thomas Telford, the great English bridge-builder,

Those great English thinkers, Hume, Smith, Reid and Duns Scotus,

Those plates which you threw out of the window are surely, in some sense, myself.

Those sad, pointless unfortunates who have never seen La Paz,

Those shits who claim my Beatrice must often shit

Those sneering perverts who say no land ever thinks itself big enough

Those who fear that, once dead, we will die further

Those who have told you, Madam, that your pubic hair

Those whom God loves and therefore causes to die in great pain,

Thou art completely bloody impossible, my dear.

Thou art the man, Odoacero. Never doubt it!

Though, alas, not quite in possession of a knack for lyricism,

Though born and raised in Tomsk, yet no-one was more Bolivian

Though he raped his own child, Daniel was at least no unbeliever;

Though I disapprove of all forms of injustice whatsoever,

Though I have spent only one hour of my life in incarceration,

Though I kept walking towards it, I never saw that spire again.

Though I regret all exploitation as being intrinsically deplorable,

Though I speak, as Paul put it, like an enormous great wambling
    buffoon,
Though I spent fifty years in Paris, O Bolivia,
Though it is scarcely my task, Great Leader, to give you advice,
Though my hand shakes uncontrollably as I write this,
Though my head shakes uncontrollably as I write this,
Though my whole body shakes uncontrollably as I write this,
Though none have called me an almost insanely great writer,
Though perhaps we cannot quite claim that Newton was Bolivian,
Though rather late, at last I found the way
Though sadly unaware of my own real sexual inclinations,
Though sinewy thighs, in the normal run of things,
Though some may claim, dear friend, that life has pissed all over you
Though something like moisture conglobes in my eyes,
Though, technically, Loch Lomond is not the largest lake in the
    world,
Though the public resonance of my work has, perhaps, been
    something less than cataclysmic
Though the struggle may not, at first sight, appear to be going
    particularly well,
Though the whole world shakes uncontrollably as I write this,
Thought is not the measure of the Universe, Otto.
Though you meditate on permanence for the next hundred years
"Thou patronising pervert!" said my love,
Three and one are the same thing, yes. However, *two*
Three lovely young shepherd boys were having a quiet toss
Three loves I have, of comfort and despair;
Three of my six favourite writers are women!
Through hole after hole the human race ascends;
Through one hole after another, life descends
Throughout the countryside, countless severe old ladies
Through the rising steam I see Mount Illimani
Thrush after thrush drops down from the leafless boughs;
Thy neat green knickers, Veronica, which a great man
Thy recent work, dear Friend, is *Shite*.
Thy unpeace, great laud God, knaught passeth comprehension;
Tibet – which, as we know, once ruled large swathes of China –
Tidy your well-lit rooms up for the better times ahead.
Tiger! Tiger! Farting uncontrollably,
Time at last to sum up all I have learned from life.

Time has a sort of magnifying glass in his pocket,
Time is an illusion – and anyway, I'm late –
Time seems to be running up that skyscraper
Time to get up again and extend my extraordinary empire.
Time wipes its tired old arse with our birth certificates.
Titia – whose tits, as a matter of fact, are the bee's knees –
To abjure the present world is to abjure reality.
Toadying up to a tyrant, and telling him he is wonderful,
To be a Christian-Cretin is my boast;
To be a convert is hardly something to boast about;
To be a tosser takes (tsk!) up my task, looks locks my tusk, an
To be Bolivian or not to be Bolivian –
To be born in Society and die in Sydney, Sidonie,
To be honest, I could have done with a bit more help.
To be honest, I had never even wanted to see her in the nude;
To be killed by a falling crucifix might, perhaps,
To be killed in the moment of one's final victory (if any)
To be murdered while still young has at least two advantages:
To be perceived requires a perceiver. Okay. So what?
To be quite frank, that angel up there worries me.
To be true, an account must first of all make sense.
To blow people up for the most moral of reasons,
To call this old jail the past seems somehow to miss the point.
"To copulate is to fail," said the mystic in the café.
Today I have farted forty-seven times in all, I think.
To deny Predestination is to deny that God
To do nothing all day but to hunt, fight and pray
To drink beer is to have failed utterly
To fight two obese giants and a dwarf simultaneously
To give people something worth talking about while they wait
To have one's arse wiped clean by the Mother of God
To "leave physical form behind" is to have ceased to exist;
To live in Oblivia is to be conscious
To Man, Nature says "F——!"
To me, the word "religion" suggests gently jiggling breasts
To Nature, Man says "F——!"
To obey the Will of God at all times is an immoral habit;
Too ill even to care what knickers my wife
To Posterity, I say only this:
To return to one's childhood religion is always a great sin.

To see the inanimate for what it really is
To see the world in a grain of opium;
To sell one's mother to the driver of a passing caravan
To sit on a mule, and fart, and think of Dante
To speak in allegories which people are *not meant* to understand
To the Ancient Celtic warriors, homosexuality
To the believer, Auschwitz must, in some final sense, be good.
To the female sex, I offer only this advice:
To the Karwendel Alps, I have only this to say:
To the Mystery of Being as Such, I say only this:
To the striking miners, I say only this: Why don't you
To think that at one time Partick was only a village!
To those sorry people who think they know everything, I say only
   this:
To those who really are evil, I have only this to say:
To understand the mystery of being might be to fail
To William Shakespeare I say this: Verbose Scotch pederast,
To women I say only this: Ungrateful, sex-mad shower
To women I say this: You have immensely
To worship God for ever? Hmm. It's a point of view.
Travelling about the country with your great legs well spread,
Treachery is, I fear, a greatly underrated quality;
Tread softly, for you tread on my enormous wobbling buttocks.
Tread softly, for you tread on my guardian angel's corns.
Tread softly, for you tread on my screams.
Trees, trees, trees, trees, trees, trees – if ever
Truly, this life is rather like a magnificent bathroom
'Truly tragic underwear'? Whenever I hear the phrase,
Truly, we belong to Nothing; and to Nothing we return.
Truth is a beautiful woman with certain problems
Try as best you can to avoid the completely fore-ordained.
Trying to flee through the jungle in a ball-gown
Try to be good, and love and help each other –
Twenty Per Cent Off Everything the sign said,
Two doors are lying on the pavement across the street;
Two hundred ships full of newly conquered slaves
Two military men, having escaped from a prison in Lima,
Two or three hundred prostitutes, whose names I have forgotten,
Two or three local prostitutes, whose names I *never knew,*

Ultimate secrets infest the earth like weeds.
Uncanny archipelago of standing stones and child molesters!
Uncle Tomas – a pathological liar, I'm afraid to say –
Unfortunately, all the wrong people died in that war.
Unfortunately, the expert was completely off his head
Unique yet strangely familiar, my second wife's private parts
Unless something else should fall on top of me,
Unlike you, I seem to earn almost obscene amounts of nothing.
Unprincipled Blockhead! Yes! Perjured Prostitute!
Unremitting rebel, whose pension from the Queen
Unutterable iteration!
Upon the platform of the Lazarus Station
Upset anyone you like except the Lividian!
Urinating in the dark does not, as such, make me happy.
Urinating out of the window of the Presidential Palace,
Uruguayan criminal! That goal was clearly offside!
Useless in bed? But I have a certificate

Vagina. Vatican City. Voltaire. Vulva.
Value my interpretation however you like, but never doubt that
Vanish into space, oh my Oblivia!
Various illegitimate (or almost illegitimate) children
Various mildly gifted thespian exhibitionists
Various parts of the Great Book were the very first (and last) to
    arrive;
Vengeance is mind, said the boa constrictor – or would have done
Verily, you have received a visit even from the Devils themselves!
Verlaine, another mellifluous Catholic pederast,
Victim though I may be of the holocaust of wind
Victorious, happy – and completely clueless –
Villain, who dares to call my Don Quixote a prancer!
Violence too must be helping to work out God's purpose.
Violent pain must, somehow, also be part of the Good Lord's
    purpose;
Virile-reviled, took-quiet-craving, sacred the veil-toque-talk revived,
Von Kundt! My God! What an absolutely *fantastic* name

Wafer all-conquering, eclipsed biscuit, yea, Christ's crisp disc, whilk
Wake up and bring thy wobbly bits to the window, Senga!
Walking back home one afternoon from the theatre, Shakespeare
Walking round sacred stones goes back a long long time.
Was I once so young? Oh, such embarrassing mistakes
Was she truly a great thinker? Well, she converted to Catholicism;
Was that a belch – or a distant door opening? (Or closing?)
Watching the pair of you lying asleep beside each other,
Watching you make up your face is worth more to me than all art,
We all have billions of years built into us;
We all have two Fates: one avoidable and one not.
We all know what it's like to fall to the floor, dead.
We appear out of slits. It is all so terribly bizarre.
    [On the other hand, how else are we supposed to get here?]
We appear out of slits. It is all so terribly bizarre.
    [On the other hand, what else are we supposed to do?]
We appear out of slots. It's all so terribly charming.
We are all, in effect, pissing into the Amazon.
We are all of us following our demolished roads.
We are clearly dealing with a major career idiot here.
We are trying to reach the Beyond by means of this rubber tube.
We cannot shriek out the word "God" often enough or loudly
    enough;
We choose Good freely; provided God has made us (do) so.
We deserve so much more than the mere unending universe.
We did it twice, didn't we?
We die; but further halfwits come along after us,
Weeds of Bolivia! (If any.)
We hardly need yet another word for sex, do we?
We have all heard the great minds farting uncontrollably;
We have often enough seen a neighbour dancing in his or her
    garden;
We know how the outer world longs to be Bolivian;
We know little of the future, but the universe knows even less,
We know the love of God is a form of vanity.
We lack most of the qualities to recognise Paradise.
We lay our thin tracing papers over the real achievements of the past,
Well? Am I Jack the Ripper, or what?
Well, at the time it was real enough, I suppose;
Well, better justice than injustice, obviously.

Well done, God! Thou certainly did the best thou couldst have done!

Well, for a start, over half the human race

Well, how exactly is nothing supposed to exist?

Well, how should I know, eh? Tell me that. How should I know?

Well, I can see how he's sadder – but how is he wiser?

Well if they have destroyed my native place, I shall just have to find myself another.

Well, I might not be God. But I am certainly jealous.

Well, I must say, the idea of God crying

Well, in a sense those works don't exist, I suppose.

Well, is it sex itself you don't like – or only sex with me?

Well, I suppose even five and a half hours in Paradise

Well, I suppose I could have done without the money worries.

Well, I suppose they at least made decent cannon-fodder

Well is your greatest river named after an ancient prostitute,

Well, it gave me something to do, I suppose.

Well, it's been very interesting – in an appalling sort of way –

Well, it's enough to be going on with, I suppose.

Well, Lord, if thou art indeed unjust, that is certainly tough on us.

Well, Madam. Would you call this a thing of beauty too?

Well, no-one can deny I have at least done the work.

Well, obviously, Christianity saved the Roman Empire.

Well, of course Celia shits. What else is she supposed to do?

Well, of course we did it. Or rather, God did it through us.

Well, that's the work more or less done. Whether anyone else is interested

Well, there's this much to be said for complete failure, I suppose:

Well, there's this to be said for falling to bits, I suppose:

Well, to kill a thousand people with an ass's jawbone

Well, two eternities are better than one, I suppose.

Well, what do you think? That the stars are deliberately doing things?

Well, which of us is saying it: You or me?

Well, who exactly would *want* to be a flea?

Well, why believe the truth when you can just continue diddling

Well, yes, thanks dear – but I already have a sister.

Well, yes – the *name* Mohammed certainly existed.

Well, you were wrong about everything – but what does that matter now?

We may be fairly certain that Adam was an African.

We may be quite sure, Kafka, that no trained gerbil
"We must learn from the past that – erm – is that my tea? –
We never hear of Jerusalem or Byzantium
We never hear of Jerusalem these days, do we?
We never met.
We never met; and yet,
We ought to have as many ways of saying "I am"
We sat half-way up an ancient sycamore
We shall never sail far away from Bailivia.
West Cunningham-Grahame Street! Can they really have largely
    demolished thee?
Western poetry as such is pretty much nothing.
We think we have nothing to do with our father's penis.
We thought that the crucial moment had come. But it hadn't.
We used to have a few of the Great Inca's letters.
We were flabbergasted in Chuqui Chuqui when first we heard
We were kept awake all night by the sound of the piping.
We were perfect together – except that we were never really happy.
We, who cannot even predict how loudly we shall fart
What a beautiful view! Hmm. Let us leave here at once –
What a complete arse God made of himself
What a damned task-mistress beauty is, O Oblivia!
What a damned task-mistress duty is, O Bolivia!
What a fantastic Universe! C——s everywhere!
What am I doing here?
What am I supposed to do? Shout through the window?
What are they doing, over there outside the Transport Museum?
What? Are they really not going to make me Emperor?
What are we all waiting for, here outside the *Museo Nacional de las
    Artes Indigenes*? Eh?
What are we supposed to learn from hallucinations?
What astonishing dreams I have in particular!
What a very ordinary little person you are, O Master!
What a wonderful idea these musical doorbells are!
What a year! First one's children. Then one's teeth.
What books should you read, my dear nephew? These fifty, above
    all else:
What can I do out here in the winter? I take off
What can I possibly say? I am eternally sorry
What can I possibly say? I am utterly devastated

What can the Devil be but one more manifestation of God?
What compensation can your f——ing ancestors give us now, Mate?
What could be more natural than for two (or perhaps three) men
What could be more wonderful
What could this be a reference to, I wonder?
What could women possibly have done to deserve flowerpots
What day is it? In fact, what year is it?
What? Did my knitting-patterns perhaps send out to their deaths
What did the ass itself make of it, one wonders?
What? Did you too not come out of a crevice?
What do all these bloody parrots think they are doing?
What does "everywhere" mean, if there's a somewhere else?
What does the date of the creation of the universe matter?
What do I intend to do? Why, nothing, of course.
What do I love most about cakes? Where should I begin?
What do I worship? Let me tell you in one word:
What do they know of Bolivia who run off somewhere else?
What do we mean when we speak of Ubelovia?
What do you mean, it's still not tomorrow?
What dreadful beards most of the great Russian writers had.
What else can one do? One just gets on with it.
Whatever else God is, Worm, he is not your personal friend.
Whatever evil God does must be called something else.
Whatever they most admire, they call "God", and suppose
What? Every human being is ultimately a Nafrican?
What exactly are you getting up to in that fine house all day?
What exactly is "a flange" anyway?
What? Face up to reality? God forbid!
What gets worshipped is usually an abuse of language.
What has a long life taught me? Absolutely nothing.
What has a long life taught me? Never tell anyone
What has a long life taught me? Perhaps this above all:
What? Has my poetry caused three Danes, two Turks and a Belgian
What I am talking about are the really good ones;
What I have between my legs has nothing to do with the public.
What I have to endure, Judas, would have killed almost anyone else.
What I like about the dead is how easily they gain weight
What I love about language is how it always lets you down.
What imaginations the builders of these religions had!
What I most dislike about him is his sheer, infinite pointlessness.

What impresses me most about Burns is that he worked for a
    living.
What is a place of worship, if not a sort of womb
What? Is docked young Dick then true, he braven whose bronzéd
    breast
What is in fact uncertain should be left uncertain.
What is it which impels the astonished nightingales to sing
What is the least important thing you can think of?
What is valuable about Faith as such? Nothing.
What? It wasn't blood after all? Dear me!
What kills us is our juvenile idealisations.
What magnificent knees that Prophet must have had
What makes us so sure that kingfishers can't fart?
What man likes to admit that the main avenue in his life
What, might I ask, is the matter with my daughter's brain?
What? Nothing broke me. I was born broken.
What Oblivia wants is, very simply, to be normal.
What on earth keeps me going? I have long since ceased to care
What one never gets to hear of are the crowds
What one so rarely sees of the past are the crowds
What one wants most are inadvertent masterpieces.
What? Only one this morning?
What other politician dared set a light to his farts in public?
"What's that?" asked God. "Sorry. I wasn't really listening."
What though it makes no sense but it be true?
What though my bones are screaming in never-ending pain?
What turd has stolen the marble and the gold
What? Was Brazil perhaps not big enough already?
What was not invented by an Oblivian?
What we need is a liberation *from* theology,
What will survive of us is a routh of bacteria
What? Will the cosmos add even more to my sufferings?
What would Jesus say? Most probably – "Go away, Gentile!"
What? You ask the reason why the soul loses its bells?
What? You dare slander the flora of Oblovia?
What you do is, you just get on with it.
What your father might have felt about your mother's arse
When Abraham saw his son shafting the angel,
When Abraham saw his son shafting the ram,
When Abraham saw the angel shafting his son,

When Abraham saw the third corpse beside him,
When another epidemic broke out in the Holy Land
When anything happens, Tim, Time exists.
When, at Hogmanay, we tried to fart out *Auld Lang Syne*,
When a woman kicks down your door at midnight, screaming,
   "Give me a bath!"
When Being itself approached me and allowed me to stand in its
   midst,
When did anyone last make his way down this path?
When did I first realise I had a heart problem?
Whenever God wonders: "Am I completely useless?"
Whenever I hear the lewd laughter of parasites,
Whenever I hear the loud laughter of priests,
Whenever I remember that the sun does not really rise,
Whenever I remember the innocent obscenities of my childhood,
Whenever I see the Emeritus Professor's lovely old Aristotle,
Whenever I think of all those millions of people
Whenever I think of world famine (and thirst)
Whenever my Fanny wrestles me to the floor,
Whenever the sun blows its nose, I think of you.
When first I saw her painting her grand-daughter's backside,
When *Freedom* came second in the 2.45 at Ayr,
When, from time to time, I sit in the bath, weeping
When God tripped over something and fell all the way down from
   Heaven,
When he became an Oblivian, perhaps in his early fifties,
When he died, I could hear a bugler playing
When he died, we could hear a bugger playing
When he who adores thee has left but his ill-fitting wig
When I am dead, I only hope they remember to destroy the right
   things;
When I came back to the flat unexpectedly with a large red cock
When I chanced to catch my love having sex with a plastic giraffe,
When I consider how your little tits,
When I consider that I have ceased to exist
When I consider that I have started to fart uncontrollably once
   again,
When I consider what a piece of crap
When I dream myself through to the other side of the All,
When I finally saw you looking underneath the bed,

When I found those dreadful pictures of my daughter's friend
When I have fears that I have missed the point,
When I heard my son say he was getting old,
When I heard that you had been unfaithful to me 643 times,
When I joked that I wished to have sex with your younger sister,
When I look at the chair in which you so often sat,
When I look back now, I see that all my teachers were cretins;
When in the tranquil night I think of Obolivia,
When I read in my mother's diaries of how, often, she used
When I saw you vomit into that plastic bag,
When I say 'the other sex', I usually mean
When I think how desperately I once needed to kiss your doormat,
When I think how many adored toys have been crushed by now,
When I think how many insults this bloody universe
When I think how often I used to lie quietly in bed in the
    morning,
When I think of all my non-existent followers
When I think, Madam, that you have taken this worthless gadget
    in your hands,
When I think of the private parts of every generation,
When I think what magnificent chestnuts your mother once had,
When it is divorced from religion, genocide
When I try to remember my last heart attack,
When I was but a little, tiny Bolivian,
When I was in Paris, it rained more or less non-stop.
When I woke up in the morning, I was suddenly deaf.
When I woke up, I saw that the statue was no longer
When I woke up that morning, I was covered in yellow fur;
When Jesus had finished juggling the loaves and fishes
When Lesbia, sneering, pulled down her little red underpants,
When lovely Miss Ferguson pissed in my flower-pot,
When my beloved asks: "Do you think I'm putting on weight?"
When my beloved refuses to lift up her thermal vest,
When my beloved says: "Don't do that again!"
When my beloved says: "Do that again!"
When my beloved says: "I think the bed's on fire,"
When my beloved says: "Never do that again!"
When my beloved says: "Will you please stop doing that?"
When my beloved sees me picking away some loose skin,
When my beloved tells me to shut up,

When, my dearest Clarinda, I vomited all over thy small, delightful
   feet,
When my dear old girl, half-drunk, flopped down naked on the
   kitchen floor,
When my delightful new girlfriend, half-drunk, brought out a pack
   of cards,
When my first wife, through a low stratagem, first caught sight of
   my private parts,
When my last hour comes and my soul fares forth in peace,
When my last hour comes and my soul farts forth in peace,
When my love calls me a disgusting pervert,
When my love said: "I think I'm having a heart-attack,"
When my love says, "I am not a National Health Psychiatrist, am I?"
When my love says, "I just *hate* those f——ing pyjamas!
When my love says, I have never had sex with a gerbil,
When my love screams: "Sit on your own f——ing face!"
When my love shrieks: "Just leave that thing alone!"
When my love's naked body was discovered 'neath the bed,
When my love starts to laugh uncontrollably,
When my love told me she had been a prostitute for eighteen
   years,
When my love whimpers: "Please get me out of this box!"
When my love whispered, "What do you think of that bust?"
When one at last reaches the stage at which a good shit
When one looks at the lands where Christianity was born
When one thinks of Jesus Christ, one rarely thinks of the pus
When people ask me what it feels like to be the greatest writer in
   the world
When she whom I worship cried: "Filthy old goat!
When the Blessed Mother of God had finally crossed her legs,
When the dear old girl finally managed to get her legs up,
When the deathbed 'convert' shouted, "Stick your sacrament up
   your arse!"
When the Divine Child bent over in the Temple
When the electric fire of Nature's plastic arm
When the girl offered her symbolic genitalia for worship
When the huge fish suddenly shot past Joshua, he fainted.
When the King refused to abandon his faith, Aladdin
When the last phallic shrine was removed from the Great Temple,
When the Mother of God almost shat herself from sheer joy,

When the public toilets are locked, the waste land nearby is,
    fortunately,
When the shivering parish priest was helped back out of the
    cupboard,
When the smiling priest asked me: "Are you impotent now too?"
When the supple nipples of the sultry deaconess
When the Talmud advises one to keep well clear of women,
When the trusted old guard at last runs off from his post,
When the white man introduced slavery into Africa
When they found another child on the uninhabited island,
When they referred to the Christian Crucifixion as "absolute
    bloody rubbish",
When three are too many, yet two are not enough,
When to sweet sessions of diving in the bushes,
When to the huge shelter of thy tiny tits
When to the sessions of sweet, silent, knicker-elastic twanging,
When we cease to exist, perhaps we enter the ultimate
When we groped each other on the stairway of the house where I
    was born
When we two farted, in silence and tears,
When we were playing cards on the sunlit patio,
When you brushed against the fresh white paint of my heart, my
    angel,
When you hear someone clambering over the roof at midnight,
When you leant against the fresh gold pain of my heart, oh my angel,
When you leapt up from the chair, shouting: "Oh, look!"
When you lie beside me in the noiselessness of the night,
When you lie to me in the noiselessness of the night,
When your father groped about with your mother's rear
When you sent me some of your dried skin through the post,
When you were playing patience on the old, sunlit piano
Whereas now we have the Divine Right of the Car Driver!
Where exactly is Scotland anyway? Here? Or here?
Where in this town can I buy authentic nomadic artefacts for cash?
Where is the Past? Which of you Gods is sitting on it?
Whether or not age in fact withered her, she is now dead.
Whether proud, or dead, or, just possibly, both,
Which is better? A handful of dirt or a handful of air?
Which of the atoms here have not been part of some people?
Which of these cities is the World Hallucination Capital?

Which of you Goddesses is sitting on the Future?
While Existence continues with its dazzling sleight of hand
While the nearby television was showing a silent film,
Who are you, fool, to point out the inadequacies
Who but an Oblivian could have invented America?
Who can know more about toothache than God himself?
Who could even imagine a world without Iblovia?
Who does not like to lie farting in bed on New Year's Day?
Who doubts that in Heaven the Gods argue in Arkadian?
Who doubts that in the Heavens the Blessed speak all our languages?
Who do you think you are, making these decisions?
Who has dared to write these 'improvements' into my manuscript?
Who has never stood trembling in the midst of Being?
Who has not had sex on the old coach-roads past the gallows?
Who has not heard of the Underpants of Damocles?
"Who is inside there? Anyone?" called out the Inca messenger.
Who is more human than a dying rubber fetishist?
Who is that first person who always walks beside you?
"Who is this Kupczyk, this vague but God-like person,
Who is this person, with the other make of private parts,
Who needs a big one when a little one works so well?
Who never ate bread that the loved one had sat on?
Whore! Absolute whore! Or, if you prefer,
Who saved the world, if not Oblivia?
Whose ancestors are we, whether we have boiled eggs or not?
Whose bowels shall sound like a harp over Moab?
Who the f—— are these children? They're not the ones I asked for.
"Who the f—— do you think you're talking to?" asked the Lord.
Who will deny that the contents of Einstein's drawers
Who would ever have guessed that I and a priestess
Who would have guessed that an Irish Anglican
Who would not be happy to die for Oblivia?
Why, after eighteen months or so, does one suddenly
Why am I loath to live in this public lavatory?
Why am I not a f——ing multi-millionaire?
Why am I sitting at this table, dissolved in tears?
Why am I so terribly tired, Pater?
Why are all these other people obsessed by sex?
Why aren't at least a few more of these people dead by now?
Why are our descendants all such tedious personages?

Why are there so many people speaking the wrong bloody language?
Why are you even alive? Any idea?
Why bother? No-one will ever notice
Why can't other people be even half as interesting as I am?
Why can't people just be nice to each other?
Why can't people just be good and kind to each other?
Why couldn't you have taken both your shoes off?
Why did it take me so long to realise
Why did My Lady tell me to "Just get lost, pronto!"
Why did that wonderful wife of mine somehow never appear?
Why did the Indian shepherd suddenly fall over again?
Why did you give me that small toy rabbit wearing only knickers?
Why did your sister refuse to sit down on my birthday cake?
Why did you suddenly vanish for almost a full year?
Why die for one's beliefs when one can kill others for them?
Why do birds have to make so much f——ing noise?
Why does Brazil not just take over the whole bloody continent?
Why does my fridge give off such a terrible smell?
Why do I find expatriate women so appallingly attractive?
Why do I have to keep hiding up in this attic?
Why do I have to speak the same language as all these stunted turds?
Why do I like you so much? I don't know. Stupidity, maybe?
Why do I suddenly feel so terribly unwell?
Why do I talk to myself so much? I'll tell you.
Why don't more women find me irresistible? In fact,
Why don't we all follow the straightest roads to our happiness?
Why don't we follow all the straight roads to our happiness?
Why do so many people write books about Paraguay?
Why, do you ask, do my anthologies contain so much of my own
    work?
Why do you have blood all over your face, Father Darwin?
Why do you keep complaining about your gorgeous little bumpers?
Why do you think I hate you? Is it because
Why exactly were those forty-odd children killed?
Why fear machines when our genitalia themselves
Why, God, are there so many bloody appalling writers?
Why go to Science when so many w——kers
Why have I turned into such a bad-tempered old bastard?
Why is everyone else so curiously limited?
Why is everything done so casually, darling?

Why is it so dark? I don't quite understand
What is it that perfectly reasonable women
Why is there a *Jack the Ripper International Airport* in Liverpool?
Why is there something rather than nothing? Well, because there
    isn't
Why is the whole world intrigued by my sexuality?
Why is this hall packed with foreign perverts?
Why, I wonder, do my dearest friends keep leaving the country?
Why not just concentrate on the real world?
Why not just try to improve what is actually in front of you?
Why not let Venezuela have a slice of our homeland too?
Why not try shoving Scottish History up your delightful arse?
Why on earth did God create so many male buttocks?
Why on earth did you call me a decrepit old lecher?
Why on earth would anyone want to work with actors?
Why read Milton when you can just shit yourself instead?
Why should complete failure have to make me completely unhappy?
Why should I care, darling, if a certain helplessness
Why should I shy away from the truth any longer?
Why shouldn't God want you to slightly deface yourself?
Why should we be in awe of so much rubbishy writing?
Why should we not suppose that the Prophets ever had diarrhoea?
Why the f—— have I taken my trousers off again?
Why worship women? Well, what else is there
Why would anyone want to go to Jerusalem?
Why would a Scandinavian want to live here at all?
Will all our descendants shit? What? Every one of them?
William Butler Yeats! Show us a card-trick.
Will the barefaced world deny us even our own slice of Antarctica?
Wilt thou lie upon thy neat back, bonnie lassie?
Wincing at yet another profound twinge at my heart
Wine, women and song – though, actually, wine and song
With a brave giggle, I fell to the ground, bleeding.
With a great cry of joy and relief, the old priest at last
With a last huge fart, he began to ascend to Heaven.
With a mind unencumbered by thoughts of mere real life,
With a sudden, ridiculous and unnecessary scream,
With chaste lips I polish the Blessed Virgin's effigy;
With joy I contemplate the fact that I shall soon be dead.
With maturity, one loses full control of one's bladder;

With maturity, one realises that woman are often dreadful too.
With me, as with Einstein, and perhaps with Leonardo da Vinci,
Without its limitations, existence would not exist.
Without the misinterpretation of images,   ·
With tears in her eyes, she repeatedly begged me
Wit? Huh. Let's leave that to Celtic pederasts.
With what astonishing grace the spiritual testicles
Woe to whoever reports the sacred texts accurately!
Woken up by her shoe landing on my foot,
Woken up yet again by an immense pain in my toenails,
Woman! For thousands of years, you have flaunted your tits;
Women and Children of Oblivia! Listen to me.
Women are quite, quite wrong to suppose that I
Women, by and large, do not like one to place explosives
Women can't possibly be as cute as that really;
Women, I am told, can be very small-minded about impotence.
Women! Is immense intelligence not what you really want?
Women's Movement, my arse. Or, perhaps more accurately,
Wonderfully combining supernaturalism and self-advertisement,
Would it help much if I added
Would we ingest, though not in jest, God's guts,
Would you believe it? The bloody thing doesn't even fit!
Wrestled into submission by your imaginary God,
Writing haiku within sight of Intillimani,
Writing haiku within sight of the Livingstone Tower,
Writing in his cell, with blankets thrown over him,

Xenophanes. Who
Xenophobia as such is entirely foreign to my nature.

Yea, God is more or less metaphorically pissing himself forever.
Yeah, yeah. That wrong-footed everyone. Including myself.
Yea, on that day God shall pull down all the underpants of those
Year after year he woke up to find himself completely unknown.
Years could surely go by with no-one venturing to this corridor,
Yes. All nearby roads lead to Rurrenabaque.

Yes, Evadne. God made everything. Nevertheless,
Yes. Here we are in Paradise. Oh, look! There's my first wife!
Yes. I know there are those who would call me bitter.
Yes, I quite like myself. Or whatever it is
Yes. I remember Achacachi.
Yes; it all starts to happen after we have ceased to exist.
Yes, I too have been kicked awake by a loved one
Yes, it would be a pity if the earth were to disintegrate
Yes. I would like to have been one of the Inca rulers.
Yes. Make yourself even more beautiful and then go out to work.
Yesterday evening, Lord, I shat about six o'clock;
Yesterday I made two very important discoveries.
Yesterday, while cleaning one of my magnificent nude crucifixes,
Yes. There are nine or ten rivers I should still like to cross;
Yes. The word 'change' stays the same, more or less. So what?
Yes. Very much so. Very, very much so.
Yes, well, at least I had the pleasure of writing it –
Yes. What I did was quite, quite, quite unforgivable.
Yes. Who needs big ones when little ones work so well?
Yes, yes. The previous women in my life
Yes. You're quite right to worship me. I'm an absolutely
    wonderful person.
Yes. Your wonderful, compassionate murals of disembowelled
    whites,
Yet again you shall be the hub of the world, oh Boulivia!
Yippee! I've got a probably fatal illness!
You are like a flower sensuously chewed by a young nun
You are well rewarded, traitor, for playing the game of the global
    bourgeoisie.
You ask, Jan, does God love your vagina? What can I reply –
You ask me what one should look for in a waning moon?
You believe against all the evidence? How immensely admirable!
You came into my life, deftly took what you wanted,
You come out here to visit me, right beside the British border,
You cried out: "How can I? All bollocks is dangerous!"
You didn't reach home, although I tried my best
You don't have to be Einstein to be dead.
You don't really doubt that I worship your foliage, do you?
You don't suppose the universe might be inside-out, do you?
You don't understand. They climb up my legs at night.

You don't yet know, O Bovelia, what a jackpot you have won!
You have been here, and here, and here so often
You know, darling, with an opening like that,
You know, Father – speaking as one pervert to another,
"You know, I could have done without that," said the Lord.
You know, if my first wife had only had a slightly bigger bust,
You know, I really thought there should be three of them.
You know, it could still turn out to be a reasonable evening.
You know, it is ever so slightly possible that I am dying.
You know, long years ago your mother sat on this very chair.
You know, that was extremely impressive, if it really happened;
You know, there are times when I can't help thinking
You know, the world is not short of lovely old drains too.
You know, to be honest, I never thought I would say this;
You know where you are with me. I have complete contempt for
    you.
You know, years ago I had your mother on this very chair.
You lived in Puerto Maldonado many years ago.
You look unbearably beautiful when you're depressed.
You might as well talk about a fart transcending the world
Young women seem not to mind my incessant rampant farting.
Young women seem to be genuinely fascinated by my dentures.
Your blood is still to some extent on my carpet.
Your buttocks, darling, are a sort of natural amphitheatre
Your cheap sneers deserve no response but contempt.
Your cheese smells absolutely wonderful, Isolde.
Your child is not you, and will not live forever either.
You realise it's all extraterrestrial, I suppose?
You're a rather nasty piece of work, wouldn't you agree?
You're dead. That's a great pity. Still: Christ died for our sins.
Your Grace, though strangely naïve sexually,
Your kitchen smells absolutely wonderful, Isolde.
Your little white knickers are the only weapons of mass destruction
Your panties, the colour of a perfect Amazonian sunset,
Your religious sentiments and your backside, Madam, I both revere.
Your strange love for Paraguayan dictators, O Caledonian bumbler,
Your threats do not frighten me. No. No. Not in the slightest.
Your whole life is the Man in the Iron Mask.
You said: "I hate it when people talk to me like that."
You sat around the whole day in a new dressing-gown;

You sat around the whole night in a lovely old dressing-gown;
You see, I am once more unexpectedly amongst you!
You shit! You have dishonoured all the women of Oblavlia!
You told me once how you killed your younger brother –
  accidentally (I think you said) –
You've had your effing chance, Mr Middle-Class Whitey!
You were wearing white in my dream. And were you covered in
  dates and figs?

Zen is, in the end, too (un)intellectual for me.
Zeo, if only the whole world were as delightful
Zubizarieta y Estigarribia! Traitor! Poof!
Zudañez! Where I saw almost the prettiest imaginable
Zzzzz. No, no. Don't wake me up. In fact,

★★★★★★★★

[END]